THE PSYCHOLOGY OF DEATH, DYING, AND BEREAVEMENT

THE PSYCHOLOGY

Richard Schulz
Carnegie-Mellon University

OF DEATH,
DYING, AND
BEREAVEMENT

ADDISON-WESLEY PUBLISHING COMPANY

Reading, Massachusetts
Menlo Park, California • London
Amsterdam • Don Mills, Ontario • Sydney

ISBN 0-201-07328-5
CDEFGHIJ-DO-79

PREFACE

This book is designed to fill an existing gap in the literature on death and dying. It presents a comprehensive review and analysis of the available empirical findings on death, dying, and bereavement. Such an analysis is possible because of the large quantities of systematic empirical data that have been collected on this topic in the last two decades. However, the usefulness of these data have in the past been limited because of the absence of an integrative review.

While some nonempirical issues are touched upon, the primary focus of this book is a critical analysis and synthesis of available data. Numerous questions and issues are raised and the relevant data are presented. When appropriate, conclusions are drawn and specific practical suggestions are made. In cases where the data do not provide the necessary information for clear-cut answers, suggestions for future research are made.

While it may be risky to claim that this book should and can be read by audiences ranging in sophistication from freshman to graduate students in psychology and professional schools, we do feel that all these groups are relevant audiences for this book. For the college student receiving her or his first exposure to this topic, this book adds an important perspective to the personal, humanistic, and philosophical views typically presented. It provides exposure to the important issues in this area and presents avenues for possible solutions to these issues. For the practitioner, this book provides an update on what we know about death, dying, and bereavement and presents suggestions for dealing with some of the problems often encountered. For the graduate student and researcher, this book makes specific suggestions for the direction of future research in this area.

An empirical perspective would be incomplete without some discussion of research methodology. This is provided in Chapter 1. Different perspectives on death and dying are described and several available research strategies are discussed. Examples from the death and dying literature are used to illustrate these various methodological approaches. While not exhaustive, this discussion provides the necessary background for those who have had little or no exposure to research methodology. For those well-grounded in research, this chapter serves as a short review of some important methodological points. Objections are often raised about the ethicality of doing research on death and dying. Chapter 1 concludes with a discussion of ethical issues and an analysis of the risks and benefits associated with the various research methodologies.

Chapters 2 through 7 comprise the substantive portion of the book, covering the major content areas. Chapter 2 examines how we think about death. An intuitive perspective is presented first and this is followed by a discussion of research on death anxiety and death fear. This research is criticized and suggestions for future research are made. Chapter 3 provides an overview on the demography of death. Questions such as what do we die of, when do we die, and where do we die are answered in this chapter. The important issues in the terminal phase of life are discussed in Chapter 4. Data on the interactions between the medical staff and the dying patient are examined; the emotional trajectory of the dying patient is described; and the needs of the dying and how they can be met are discussed. The chapter concludes with an examination of the euthanasia issue and with a discussion of some of the recent perspectives on the definition of death.

While most of this book deals with psychological aspects of dying, Chapter 5 is concerned with psychological aspects of living. Social psychological and biological determinants of longevity are discussed with the aim of identifying those variables that are likely to both improve the quality and increase the duration of life.

"How do we respond to the death of someone close to us?" is the question addressed in Chapter 6 on grief and bereavement. Data on the physiological and behavioral consequences of bereavement are examined and the effectiveness of various therapeutic procedures available to the bereaved are discussed.

The final chapter is devoted to death education. Examples of several death education programs that are directed at a variety of audiences ranging from children to medical practitioners are presented.

Pittsburgh, Pa.   R. S.
March 1978

ACKNOWLEDGMENTS

Acknowledgments are due many people who participated in the preparation of this manuscript. First and foremost I am grateful to Elaine Shelton for her help in organizing and editing the manuscript. Betsy Lyden, Ed Sieger, and Muriel Fleishman deserve credit for typing and retyping this manuscript. Among the persons who reviewed various earlier versions of this book, I am thankful to my students at Carnegie-Mellon University, who provided valuable feedback; to Robert Kastenbaum, who has been a model throughout my career and who provided valuable criticisms; and to Mary Ann Watson and Larry Bugen, whose suggestions improved the manuscript significantly.

I bring a particular perspective to this topic and, while its value may be debatable, I am personally grateful to my teachers at Duke University for giving me the opportunity to acquire it. Included among these are David Aderman, Jack Brehm, Edward E. Jones, George Maddox, and Susan Roth. I am especially grateful to David Aderman who aroused my interest in this area and who collaborated with me on many death projects. To those too numerous to mention who provided enough diversion to make writing this manuscript a work of love, I give my love. Finally, Robert Rosenbaum deserves credit for proving to me once again that if you want something done right, you'd better do it yourself. Last but not least, a hearty thanks to Michael Scheier, who in the end proved to have helped slightly more than he hindered. Preparation of this book was in part supported by Grant 00525 from the National Institute on Aging.

CONTENTS

1

INTRODUCTION: GENERAL ISSUES AND RESEARCH STRATEGIES

Interest in death, dying, and bereavement has grown in a variety of disciplines in the last two decades. The psychologist's involvement in and contributions to these areas are reflected in the recent proliferation of books, journals, classes, and research centers devoted to psychological aspects of death, dying, and bereavement. Perhaps the most telling evidence for the widespread popularity of these topics is the amount of coverage given them by the media. Articles in newspapers and popular magazines, television talk shows, and documentaries focusing on findings and opinions on death and dying are common. Whether this widespread interest will continue remains to be seen.

My best guess is that it will continue—and indeed grow—in the years to come. Why should this be the case? The answer is found in part in the nature of the controversial issues popularized by the media. While many new areas, from the plight of the terminal patient to the relationship between bereavement and mortality, have been examined, the focus has been on a variety of problems that have been with us for many years but have only recently been openly scrutinized. How does one define death? What is the psychological impact of a terminal illness on the patient and his or her family? Should a doctor tell the truth to a terminal patient? Interest in death and dying should persist as long as these problems persist, and it is unlikely that they will vanish on their own. Research and discussion of these problems should continue and expand as long as we believe that something can be done about them. Once they are solved or we conclude that they are insoluble, concern may quickly wane.

The new interest in death and dying is also attributable to the increased attention paid to the processes and problems of aging. Since death is a frequent occurrence among the aged, the problems of death and dying are often viewed as a subclass of problems within aging. The prognosis for the field of aging is similarly positive; thus we should see an increase in research and popular discussions of this topic.

Finally, credit is due to some specific researchers and writers, who through their work have brought the topic of death and dying to the attention of the public. Individuals like Elizabeth Kübler-Ross (1969) and Herman Feifel (1959) have aroused enough public interest in the area to warrant frequent newspaper and popular magazine articles. As a result of her innovative work with terminal patients, Dr. Cicely Saunders (Holden, 1976) has likewise been effective in bringing the problems of dying to the attention of the public. And we should add to this list the innumerable scientists who studied and wrote about death and dying long before it became popular to do so. Such a list would be too long to include here but I hope to do them justice by citing their work in the pages that follow.

PERSPECTIVES ON DEATH, DYING, AND BEREAVEMENT

While many writers and researchers still insist that death is a subject that is evaded, ignored, and denied, the volumes of written material published on the topic argue against them. Death has been pricked, punctured, dissected, inspected, and analyzed from almost every perspective. Library shelves are filled with books on the philosophical, religious, sociological, anthropological, psychological, and medical views of death. Journal articles frequently appear with titles such as "Death in Art," "Death in Literature," "Death in Music," and so on. To this list we can add the numerous published personal accounts of the terminal phase of life and discussions of phenomena such as life after death.

Widespread interest in death is not a particularly recent phenomenon. For philosophers and theologians death has been a concern for centuries. From Epicurus (352-270 B.C.) to Bertrand Russell, the significance of death to man's existence has been one of the major focal points of philosophical thought and writing. The meaning of death for mankind is the point of embarkation for the existentialist philosophies of Heidegger and Sartre. Death appears often in literature. Every serious writer of the last three centuries has been concerned at one time or another with death, dying, nonexistence, life after death, and so on. It appears that death is indeed more pervasive as a topic than most writers have thus far acknowledged.

But there is a qualitative difference between the approaches taken in the last two decades as compared to earlier treatments of this topic. For the first time, investigators in a variety of disciplines have endeavored to collect systematic, empirical data. Much of the data-gathering has been stimulated and carried out by psychologists, but professionals in other disciplines such as sociology, anthropology, and medicine have participated as well. The methodological techniques used to collect data have varied widely and speculation has often gone far beyond the data. There is a growing consensus that large quantities of empirical data are required for answers to the many problems already identified (e.g. what are the psychological needs of the terminal patient?). For some problems we have already collected sufficient information to make some tentative suggestions for solutions. For example, we know enough about the interactions between medical staff and dying patients to make specific suggestions to medical caretakers regarding their treatment of the terminally ill. We also know enough about the bereavement processes to specify the types of intervention needed in particular cases.

For other death-related problems, the data do not provide the necessary information to make clear-cut decisions. The data do, however, offer information that should allow for more intelligent decisions. The issue of whether or not to inform the dying patient of her or his terminality is a case in point. The available evidence on this question does not provide us with a pat answer, but it does tell us what the important aspects of that issue are. Finally, research findings may not provide an immediate answer to a question, but instead indicate where to look next. The usefulness of these large quantities of empirical literature is unfortunately limited because of the unavailability of comprehensive reviews and analyses of the relevant literature. This book is intended to correct this situation. While some nonempirical issues are touched upon here, the primary aim is to present a comprehensive review and analysis of the available empirical findings on death, dying, and bereavement.

My use of the term "empirical" has thus far been vague. In the following section, the meaning of empirical data is more clearly defined; methods used to collect data are discussed; and the advantages and disadvantages of the available research methodologies are examined.

THE EMPIRICAL APPROACH

Empirical knowledge is knowledge based on observation or experiment. The method of observation may be very systematic, involving several observers and many subjects, or it may involve only one observer who casually notes the behavior of one or more persons. An experiment is a formal test of a specific hypothesis that relates a series of events to a particular outcome. The important difference between empirically based and nonempirical methods is that in empirical research, descriptions and explanations of events are based on data gathered from the individuals we are studying, while the nonempirical approach might rely more heavily on armchair conjecture or personal intuition. This does not mean that empirically based observations or explanations are necessarily more accurate than those derived via armchair philosophizing. The empirical approach does, however, represent a commitment to testing and continued reevaluation of observations and explanations. In the long run, our understanding of various phenomena should be more accurate than it would be had we used nonempirical methods.

Three types of empirical approaches are generally available to the researcher: observational, correlational, and experimental. Each of these is discussed in detail below and appropriate examples of each that were taken from the death and dying literature are described.

Observational methods

The simplest data gathering technique is to observe the behavior of one or more individuals, describe it, and perhaps venture some explanation for the observed behavior. The simplest form of observation is the *case study*. Typically, case studies are detailed descriptions of one individual. The description may be based on a formal interview with the person or the individual may be unobtrusively observed (that is, without his or her knowledge) in a variety of settings. If we have some base-rate information (data on average behavior of a population), we can compare our observations with those standards to determine where the individual falls on some dimension.

Although it is difficult to derive general conclusions from single case studies, they are a valuable source for hypotheses and conjectures about human behavior. These conjectures can then be further tested by interviewing and observing more individuals. The data obtained from such interviews are typically not quantitative (that is, adaptable to numerical or statistical analysis). They consist of impressions, specific detailed descriptions, and often a great deal of speculation. It is therefore difficult to analyze these data using the available statistical procedures.

The work of Elizabeth Kübler-Ross represents this approach. She was initially confronted by four theology students who wanted to examine death as a crisis in human life. After much discussion, it became clear to them that it would be almost impossible to use traditional scientific procedures involving the collection and verification of data. Instead, they decided simply to observe critically ill patients—"study their responses and needs, evaluate the reactions of the people around them, and get as close to the dying as they would allow us" (Kübler-Ross, 1969, p. 22). Several hundred patients were eventually interviewed. On the basis of these interviews, Kübler-Ross concluded that terminal patients, if given enough time, pass through five distinct stages (denial, anger, bargaining, depression, and acceptance) from the time they learn of their condition to their death.

It is important to note that Kübler-Ross's *stages theory* is based on the impressions of one individual. No attempt was made to control or systematize the interview process or to check the reliability of the observations. Given these limitations, her conclusions are perhaps best viewed as hypotheses rather than as guides for policy formation. More sophisticated investigations are necessary to adequately evaluate speculations such as these. A more detailed discussion of this material is presented in Chapter 5.

Nardini's observation of American prisoners of war (cited in Le Shan, 1961) is another example of the observational method in action. According to Nardini, death in a prison camp was more likely to be related to the individual's will to live, or level of hope, than his physical condition. As with Kübler-Ross's work, these are impressionistic data in need of validation.

In general, data obtained through observational methods are best viewed as a source of provocative hypotheses. The opportunities for bias in collecting such data are too great to warrant an easy acceptance of theories or hypotheses based solely on observational data.

Correlational methods

When an investigator is interested in measuring the relationship between two variables, she or he computes the correlation between the two variables—that is, she or he assesses the extent to which variations in one variable are related to variations in the other variable. A simple example is the relationship between weight and height. If we measure the weights and heights of 100 individuals and graphed them, we would find that as height increases so does weight. Thus, height and weight are positively correlated. An example of negative correlation is the relationship between age and strenuous physical activity among adults. For most persons, as age increases physical activity decreases.

The end product of a correlational analysis is a *correlation coefficient*, which is a number ranging from −1 to +1, reflecting the degree of relationship between two variables. The sign (positive or negative) reflects the direction of the relationship, and the deviation from 0 indicates the strength of the relationship. A correlation of +0.89, for example, means that the relationship between two variables is positive (when one increases or decreases, so does the other) and quite strong. A correlation of +1.00 is a perfect positive correlation, indicating that as one variable increases at a constant amount, so does the other variable. A perfect negative correlation (−1.00) means that the higher the value of one variable, the lower the value of the other. Perfect correlations, either positive or negative, are rarely found. A correlation of 0.00 indicates that there is no relationship between the two variables.

How has this tool been used by death researchers? Correlational methods are frequently used by investigators interested in the relationship between death anxiety (as measured by a death anxiety scale) and a wide assortment of demographic and personality variables. Dozens of studies have examined the relationship between death anxiety (DA) and sex, age, religious beliefs, education, and so on. A question frequently asked about religiosity and DA is, "Do individuals who are very religious have less death anxiety?" While the findings are not very clear-cut (see Chapter 2 for a detailed discussion), there is some evidence showing that the correlation between DA and degree of religiosity is negative—that is, the more religious the individual, the lower the DA. Another popular example from the death literature is the relationship between hopelessness and physical decline. Negative correlations have been found between the level of hopelessness and the length of survival. The more hopeless a patient feels, the faster his or her decline and the sooner death occurs.

The careless researcher might infer from this correlation that hopelessness *causes* physical decline. This is a logical and reasonable conclusion to draw, but it is incorrect if based only on correlational data. Correlation does *not* imply causation. It is impossible to determine from a simple correlation whether one variable caused the other or vice versa, or whether a third variable is involved, which may be correlated with both. In the example presented above, we cannot determine whether hopelessness caused the physical decline or whether the patient's awareness of her or his physical decline caused the hopelessness.

Finally, it is possible that a third variable is involved, such as the physician's attitude regarding the patient's prognosis. A physician may become hopeless about the patient's prospect for recovery, and this attitude may be conveyed to the patient, causing him or her to become hopeless as well. Furthermore, a physician may stop certain treatment procedures because of his or her hopelessness, causing the patient to die sooner than expected. This is a purely speculative example, but it illustrates the fallacy of deriving causal explanations from correlational data. Under some circumstances, it may be possible to derive causal relationships from correlational data, but these circumstances are quite rare. A more effective means for determining causality is to use experimental methods.

Experimental methods

Instead of waiting or searching for naturally occurring situations, a researcher can sometimes control or create the conditions necessary for studying a particular relationship. She or he can, in short, carry out an *experiment*. The experimental approach has several specific advantages over descriptive or correlational approaches. First, the experimenter can set up the conditions necessary for studying the phenomenon of interest. Second, the experimenter can vary the conditions, making it possible to assess the impact of various levels of one variable on some other variable. Third, the experimenter can randomly assign subjects to conditions, thereby eliminating the confounding effects of prior differences among subjects. The combined effect of these three advantages is that the experimenter can make causal inferences about the variables of interest.

All experiments have several features in common. An experimenter typically begins with a specific hypothesis that relates one variable to another variable. Recall the previously described relationship between hopelessness and physical decline. On the basis of the observed correlation between these variables, the experimenter might decide to test the hypothesis that increased hopelessness causes faster physical decline. For obvious ethical reasons, the experimenter can test only the complementary hypothesis—that decreased hopelessness, or increased hopefulness, causes slower physical decline. The variable to be manipulated becomes the *independent variable*. In our example, this would be the level of hope. To assess the impact of the level of hope on some outcome variable, we must have at minimum two levels of hope. We might, for example, have one condition in which subjects are given information designed to make them more hopeful and another condition in which no such information is given.

The outcome, or *dependent variable*, is the rate of physical decline. With the independent and dependent variables specified, we can now search for an appropriate population, randomly assign subjects to conditions, carry out the manipulation, and measure the rate of physical decline. Assuming that everything is well-executed and finding that those subjects who were made more hopeful lived longer, we can now conclude that the level of hope is causally related to physical decline. Making individuals more hopeful causes them to live longer.

Experimental research is generally more difficult and costly to carry out than other types of research. It would require too much space to discuss in detail the many problems unique to the experimental approach, but one issue deserves coverage in even this brief discussion—that issue is *ethics*. Ethical issues are perhaps most salient in the context of experimental research, but these issues should be considered in all types of research.

RESEARCH PROGRESS AND ETHICS

It was pointed out earlier that research on the psychological aspects of death, dying, and bereavement has proliferated in the last two decades. Much of this research has been descriptive or correlational, and it may be argued that in the beginning stages of knowledge-gathering within an area, nonexperimental methods are highly desirable and even preferable. Under some circumstances, these are the only methods that can be used. It is only when questions of causality are raised that experimental or, in some cases, sophisticated correlational approaches become necessary.

As research within an area progresses from the descriptive to the correlative and finally to the experimental phase, ethical issues become more important as the potential for harm to subjects increases. No matter what method is used, however, important ethical issues are raised when carrying out research in this area. For the most part, the ethical issues concern the consent and debriefing of subjects, and the assessment of the risk-benefit ratio. These issues are presented schematically in the context of the three types of research strategies given in Fig. 1.1.

Type of study	Type of consent	Type of debriefing			Cost/Benefit analysis		
		None	False/Partial	Complete	Direct personal benefit	Direct personal risk	Societal benefits
Observational	None						
	False/Partial				Low	Low	Low
	Complete						
Correlational	None						
	False/Partial				Moderate	Moderate	Moderate
	Complete						
Experimental	None						
	False/Partial				High	High	High
	Complete						

Fig. 1.1
A schematic presentation of three types of research methods and the relevant ethical issues.

Consent

The left column in Fig. 1.1 shows the three types of studies to be examined. Moving from left to right, we note that for each type of study a researcher may or may not decide to obtain consent or permission to collect data from the participants in the study.

Three types of consent are possible. A researcher may decide not to obtain consent. This is relatively easy to accomplish when carrying out observational studies. A researcher observes individuals unobtrusively or can collect observational data in the context of providing some service. A physician may, for example, record her or his observations of terminal patients while treating them. In most situations, it is mandatory that the subject not know he or she is being observed. Informing the subject or obtaining consent may significantly change his or her behavior, making the validity of the observation suspect. The ethical issue involved here is relatively minor. It may be argued that observing another without informing him or her is an invasion of privacy. However, it would be difficult to support this argument without restricting many aspects of human behavior in general.

Obtaining consent from research participants is a more serious issue when carrying out correlational and experimental studies. It is reasonably easy to carry out correlational studies and not obtain consent. Research based on archival data (e.g., information obtained from public records such as death certificates) is a good example.

Phillips and Feldman (1973) used archival data to test the relationship between birthdates and deathdates. These data were obtained from "Four Hundred Notable Americans," a biographical appendix to *The Encyclopedia of American History* (1965). Analysis of the data revealed a significant death dip before birthdays. That is, fewer people than expected died before their birthdays, suggesting that people were able to postpone their deaths until after their birthdays. From an ethical perspective, it was obviously impossible for Phillips and Feldman to obtain permission from anyone to test the relationship between birthdates and deathdates. The data were part of the public domain and therefore available to everyone.

A great deal of correlational evidence is based on interview or questionnaire data obtained directly from individuals. Under these circumstances, the researcher must gain either false, partial, or complete consent from the subject. False consent is obtained when the researcher deceives the subject about the intent of an interview or questionnaire. Another possibility is that the researcher only partially informs the subject about the intent of the research project. The subject may therefore agree to participate, but may not be fully aware of why particular kinds of data are being collected or what the researcher's real hypotheses are. It may be necessary to get consent by giving subjects only false or partial information in situations where awareness of the real hypothesis would influence the subject's response.

This problem frequently occurs in experimental studies. For example, a researcher may be interested in the effects on death anxiety (DA) of a course dealing with the topic of death and dying. To test this hypothesis, the experimenter might administer DA scales before and after the course to one group of students in the course and to another group who did not participate. The hypothesis might be that students who took the course will show a decline in DA from pretest to post-test relative to those who did not take the course. Clearly, the validity of such a result would be questionable if the experimenter explained the full intent of his or her research. Subjects typically are very obliging and as a result may change their responses to confirm the researcher's hypothesis. This problem can be avoided by imbedding the items of the DA scale in a larger questionnaire and contriving a story about the research that does not sensitize subjects to the real purpose of the experiment.

Experimental research is rarely carried out without some form of consent from the subjects. The one exception that comes to mind is the naturally occurring experiment. Occasionally, a researcher can take advantage of a naturally occurring event and treat it as a manipulation.

For example, a researcher may hypothesize that having something positive to look forward to causes terminal patients to become more hopeful and thus live longer. An improved institutional environment may be the kind of positive event that would serve as the manipulation. While it may not be possible to bring about the renovation of an institution for the purposes of an experiment, such events do occur naturally and can be used as manipulations when they occur. By comparing the length of survival of persons who were admitted several months before the renovations (who thus had the opportunity to look forward to the new environment) to individuals admitted shortly after the renovations were completed, we can determine the impact of positive future events.

Such studies clearly do not permit the kind of control necessary for true experiments. Often many assumptions have to be made (or checked out) for the data to be meaningful. Nevertheless, the researcher should keep her or his eyes open for the opportunity to carry out such studies. Many of the ethical issues inherent in true experimental designs are avoided with this type of research.

Debriefing

After the data have been collected, the researcher may spend some time with the subject explaining the true nature of the research project and the reasons for various aspects of the study, such as why certain questions were asked, why they were deceived if deception was used, and so on. This process is called *debriefing*. Three types of debriefing are possible: none, false/partial, and complete.

Briefly, in a complete debriefing, the study participant is told everything about the study. When the subject is given false or only partial information about a study, he or she has received a false/partial debriefing. Finally, a subject may not be debriefed at all. How do each of these debriefing strategies apply to the three research methodologies?

Whether or not a subject is debriefed should depend, in part, on whether his or her consent was obtained to collect data. Debriefing is by definition unnecessary when the subject's consent is based on complete knowledge of the study. Under these circumstances there is nothing to debrief the subject about; she or he already knows everything there is to know. The issue becomes more complex in studies where subjects were not asked for their consent or gave their consent under false pretenses. In some situations it would make little sense to debrief a subject who was not asked to give his or her consent for participating in a study. In most observational, correlational, and experimental studies in which the participant is not aware that she or he is being observed, debriefing may do more harm than good. It may confuse and upset the subject. In the quasi-experimental study described earlier where the effect of having something positive to look forward to was assessed, debriefing would clearly be inappropriate. Informing subjects that the researcher was interested in their length of survival could be misinterpreted by patients and cause much anxiety among them.

A correlational study by LeShan (Kastenbaum and Aisenberg, 1972) provides another example of a study where debriefing would be inappropriate. LeShan observed nurses caring for patients of varying health status. Using a stop watch, he recorded the length of time it took a nurse to respond to terminal and nonterminal patients and found that the time for responding to terminal patients was longer than for nonterminal patients. Obtaining informed consent for this study might very well have affected the behavior of the nurses and debriefing them afterwards might have upset them. These dilemmas can be avoided by not carrying out this type of research in the first place, but that would place severe limitations on what we can study.

Observational and correlational studies based on archival data preclude the possibility of debriefing, as well as the need for consent. Just as Phillips was unable to gain consent from his subjects in the birth-date-deathdate study, he was unable to debrief them.

The problems of debriefing become most serious in studies where the subject consented to participate when given false or partial information. On the one hand, the researcher is ethically obligated to explain the real reason for carrying out such a study. On the other hand, it may be upsetting for the subject to discover that she or he has been deceived and/or has behaved in an embarrassing or negative manner.

These problems can be avoided if great care is used in planning and executing the debriefing. In general, a successful debriefing should accomplish three things. First, it should reduce any anxiety created by participating in the study. A participant's level of anxiety should be no higher after completing the experiment than it was before the experiment. Second, the participant's level of self-esteem and sense of well-being should not be lowered as a result of participating in the study. Third, the debriefing should impart information about the reasons and significance of a particular study as well as the nature of scientific inquiry in general. Needless to say, accomplishing these goals requires both foresight and sensitivity. In general, research that requires deception should be used only as a last resort and when such research is necessary it should be carried out by experienced professionals.

RISK-BENEFIT ANALYSIS

A question raised throughout this and subsequent chapters is, "Should certain potentially harmful types of research be carried out?" Assuming that a research project is operationally feasible, a partial answer to this question can be found by doing a risk-benefit analysis—that is, by stacking up the potential risks of a study (harm to the subject) against the potential benefits and determining which comes out higher. Since these are inherently subjective judgments, committees have been established within universities and government agencies to help make these decisions.

As Fig. 1.1 indicates, a study can be assessed in terms of two types of benefits and one type of risk. A study may provide direct personal benefits to the participant, and it may provide general knowledge that may be useful to society as a whole. The risk involves the possibility of psychological harm to the study participant. A subject may become embarrassed or have his or her self-worth threatened as a result of participating in a study.

Figure 1.1 also indicates the relationship between risks, benefits, and method of research. Although there are exceptions, it can be argued that both risks and benefits are generally low for observational research, moderate for correlational research, and highest for experimental research. This generalization is made for two reasons.

First, the probability of personal contact on a one-to-one basis increases as one moves from observational to correlational to experimental studies. Observational research is often carried out without actually interacting with the participants. Thus, the chances of doing harm are less, but so are the chances of providing direct personal benefits. With experimental research, it is typically necessary to interact with a subject on a one-to-one basis to collect data and/or carry out the manipulation. This can be beneficial in several ways. A subject may be flattered by the attention given him or her, and may feel good about making a valuable contribution to science. The subject's sense of self-worth may be enhanced if given the opportunity to state his or her opinions. And, finally, the subject may gain some insight into himself or herself and the surrounding world.

On the other hand, direct personal risk is higher when using the experimental method. The self-insight gained may be negative. Subjects may feel less competent than they thought they were or they may behave in an embarrassing manner. Although precautions can be taken to avoid these outcomes, the risk of their occurrence is still clearly higher in experiments than in observational or correlational studies.

Finally, we have argued that society's benefits vary as a function of the method used, with correlational and experimental research providing relatively more benefits than observational research. The reasons for this are found in the kinds of answers each type of research strategy provides. Observational studies are a good source of ideas or hypotheses about the world. However, their validity is often suspect and it would be risky indeed to base policy that affects human lives on them. Correlational research is somewhat more useful. Given that we know the degree of the relationship between two or more variables, we may, in some cases, be able to make reasonable judgments about the direction of causality. Policy is very often based on this type of data, especially in problem areas where it is impossible to carry out experimental research. Finally, experimental research typically provides the most useful data for the understanding of human phenomena because it can isolate causal agents. It is relatively easy to translate the results of experiments, especially when they are carried out in a real-world setting, into policy decisions that will have predictable effects on a particular population.

CONCLUSION

We have examined three general research strategies and illustrated how they might be applied to study the psychology of death, dying, and bereavement. Most of the data in this book are based on observational and correlational techniques. These research methods have been fruitful in providing many provocative hypotheses relevant to the study of death and dying. As is true with most growing disciplines the questions by far outnumber the answers. Finding some of these answers will depend on our willingness to adopt experimental methods of research. Throughout this book, suggestions are made as to the types of experimental designs needed to answer particular questions. The decision to carry them out should be based on a careful assessment of the potential risks and benefits involved. Different readers will reach different conclusions, but we should all be aware of the options available to us.

2

THINKING ABOUT DEATH

AN INTUITIVE PERSPECTIVE

"Of all things that move man, one of the principle ones is his terror of death" (Becker, 1973). This statement is the premise of Ernest Becker's provocative book, *The Denial of Death*. Becker argues that "the idea of death, the fear of it, haunts the human animal like nothing else; it is a mainspring of human activity—activity designed largely to avoid the fatality of death, to overcome it by denying in some way that it is the final destiny for man" (Becker, 1973). While Becker argues his case better than most, he would be the first to admit that his basic premise is not a particularly new slant on the significance of death to man's existence. How to deal with the end of life has been a major focus of all contemporary and ancient religions and the central problem of philosophers from Epicurus of Ancient Greece to Heidegger and the modern existentialists.

It would be impossible to review here the innumerable views of death proposed in humanity's recorded history. Most writers would agree on one point, however—*death is a paradox*. Death is both a destructive and creative force. The basic premise of the paradox is that human beings fear or are anxious about death, and it is this fear or anxiety that directly and indirectly motivates much of their behavior. On the one hand, fear of death has been identified as the genesis of neurosis (Meyer, 1975) and psychosis (Becker, 1973); on the other hand, the pleasure of existence and many of humanity's good works have been attributed to the fear of death.

One might ask, do people really fear death and, if so, what exactly do people fear about death? With the exception perhaps of Gary Gilmore, a convicted murderer who recently asked to be executed, it is reasonable to assume that most people in Western society consider death, at best, a mediocre experience. Although the supporting data are not available, it is likely that death is not on our minds much of the time and for most persons it looms far enough in the future that we experience little anxiety over the prospect of dying and being dead. On the other hand, death is an experience that few people seek out. We are, in fact, willing to spend fortunes to avoid it. The question to be answered then is, "What is it about death that makes it such an undesirable prospect?" Anyone can easily generate at least a partial list in answer to this question. The reader may be surprised to find how long this list can actually get.

In brief, the negative aspect of death and dying can be classified under two general and interactive categories—psychological and physical suffering. They are interactive because each can intensify the other and neither exists in isolation.

Fear of physical suffering

As the causes of death change in our society so does the probability of experiencing physical discomfort. Chapter 3 shows how slow degenerative processes, such as cancer, are more often the cause of death today than they were 50 years ago. While it is possible to control the pain often associated with cancer, the best methods available are not always used. We have all heard stories of persons with terminal cancer who experienced months and sometimes years of excruciating pain before death. A related concern that has elements of both physical and psychological suffering is the deterioration of the body that is sometimes a consequence of a degenerative disease such as cancer. Breasts or limbs are removed, lesions develop that don't heal, and body systems cease to function normally. An individual who has lived an active and vital life can be easily devastated by such events, and for those of us who are presently healthy and vigorous the thought of such deterioration can be frightening indeed.

Fear of humiliation

This is a purely psychological fear, but it is often born out of physical suffering. It is the fear of becoming a coward in the face of death either because of the physical suffering (e.g., pain) we might experience or because we dread the thought of not existing—i.e., of being dead.

Interruption of goals

For some individuals, the thought of death is anxiety-arousing because death will interfere with the achievement of their goals. Length of life is often measured in terms of accomplishments rather than in absolute time. This is particularly true for academics. When asked how long he or she wants to live, a university professor might reply, "long enough to write two more books." More mundane examples can be found in our own personal experiences and the interview protocols reported by Kübler-Ross. Persons who are old or severely ill often talk about living long enough to experience a particular event such as a birthday, wedding, anniversary, and so on. Thus, people may become fearful or anxious if they feel that death might deny them the opportunity to achieve certain goals or to experience particular events.

Impact on survivors

Another source of death anxiety might be the psychological and economic impact of one's death on emotionally involved survivors. The parent with a large family depending on him or her for economic and emotional support may worry about the impact of his or her death on the children. It could be argued that purchasing life insurance is one way of "buying off" some of this death anxiety.

Fear of punishment

Religious people, who have a strong belief in an afterlife in which one atones for deeds committed while living, may fear the prospect of being punished for misdeeds. As our society continues to become more secularized, however, this source of death anxiety should decline.

Fear of not being

"Man is the only creature who must live with the constant awareness of the possibility and inevitability of nonbeing" (Coleman, 1972, p. 71). Unless an individual chooses suicide, she or he must live with the fact that death will come at some unknown time and place. According to existentialist thinkers, it is this awareness of inevitable death that leads us to existential anxiety—a deep concern over the meaning of life. This concern manifests itself through questions about whether one is leading a fulfilling and authentic life. Viewed from the existential perspective, the idea of nothingness can arouse anxiety so general that it influences our entire lives.

Fear of the death of others

All of the possible sources of fear and anxiety described up to now are reasons why we might fear our own death. However, we may also fear the death of those around us. We may become anxious at the thought of having to experience vicariously the psychological and physical suffering of those close to us. In addition, we might fear the loss of an important relationship. To the extent that we perceive an individual as a source of many of our positive outcomes, we should dread that person's death.

FEAR AND ANXIETY

The terms fear and anxiety have been used here interchangeably. A distinction often made by psychoanalysts is that *fear* is experienced in reference to specific environmental events or objects, while *anxiety* is a negative emotional state that lacks a specific object. The apprehension evoked by thoughts of death and dying has properties of both fear and anxiety. There are specific things one can fear, such as the pain and associated psychological suffering. In addition, thinking about death may arouse amorphous and unspecified anxieties about the many unknowns associated with death—that is, we do not know when, where, or how we will die, or if there is an afterlife. The idea of *not being* is for some persons incomprehensible and unsettling.

Since specific fears are grounded in the environment, they are amenable to treatment. For example, people's fears of the pain of dying may be eliminated if they can be asssured that appropriate drug-therapies will be made available to them should they become terminal. Similarly, the knowledge that dying persons are treated with respect and compassion may reduce the fear of an undignified death. The fact that these fears still exist lends credence to the argument that these are problems in our culture, and it is one of the goals of this book to identify and suggest solutions to these problems. (See Chapter 4 for a more detailed discussion of these topics.)

Death anxiety is a much stickier problem. Clearly, it is ethically impossible to specify the time, place, and manner of death for most persons. Nor is it possible to convincingly demonstrate what it is like to be dead, although some persons claim to have knowledge of this (see R. Moody, *Life After Life*, 1976). Most likely we will never be able to do anything about these causes of anxiety.

While this anxiety may be a burden, it may also be a great boon to humanity. According to the psychoanalyst Zilboorg (1943), the behaviors and psychological energies invested in self-preservation are products of death anxiety. Most of the time, these anxieties are repressed and must remain repressed if we are to function normally, but they exist and, like boiling water in a teapot, exert their pressures on man's behavior. When the pressures become too great and the pot boils over, the anxieties manifest themselves in neurotic and psychotic behaviors (Becker, 1973; Meyer, 1975). Taking this perspective to the extreme, one might argue that many of humanity's great individual achievements may be attributable to death anxiety. Becker (1973) argues fervently that many of humanity's heroic achievements represent an attempt to master this anxiety and conquer death. Most of us know persons who are motivated to transcend their physical mortality through their products—e.g., the artist who hopes her or his work will live forever or the politician who wants his or her accomplishments recorded in history books.

While this view of death anxiety may have some intuitive appeal, little research is available to either refute or support it. Indeed, it may be impossible to test many of these notions using empirical methods, and it can perhaps be argued that some of these ideas were never meant to be tested empirically. Nevertheless, while literature abounds with speculation about the nature and meaning of death, we also have available large quantities of research on death anxiety. This literature is examined next.

DEATH ANXIETY RESEARCH

Death anxiety has been measured in a variety of populations and settings with a wide assortment of assessment devices ranging from projective techniques (such as the Rorschach and Thematic Apperception Test) to the measurement of galvanic skin response, a physiological correlate of anxiety. It is the aim of this review to bring order to the existing death anxiety literature and direction to the field by critically evaluating the various methods used to assess death anxiety, deriving conclusions warranted by the available data, and suggesting the direction that future research should follow. Before this literature is examined, one qualifier is in order. The distinction between *death fear* and *death anxiety* described earlier has not been made by empirical researchers. As a result, the two terms are used interchangeably in the discussion that follows.

Methodological issues

Both direct and indirect techniques have been used to assess death anxiety. Direct techniques include questionnaires, check lists, and rating scales, while indirect techniques include projective tests, the measurement of galvanic skin response, and reaction times during death-related work association tasks. Direct techniques are by far the more frequently used, and at present there are six widely used death anxiety questionnaires (Boyar, 1964; Collett and Lester, 1969; Lester, 1967a; Sarnoff and Corwin, 1959; Templer, 1970; Tolor, 1967).

An example of one death anxiety scale is presented in Table 2.1. After reading each statement, the respondent decides for him- or herself whether a particular statement is true or false. These responses are then coded according to a key, and a death anxiety score is derived.

TABLE 2.1 *Templer's Death Anxiety Scale.*

Content
I am very much afraid to die.
The thought of death seldom enters my mind.
It doesn't make me nervous when people talk about death.
I dread to think about having to have an operation.
I am not at all afraid to die.
I am not particularly afraid of getting cancer.
The thought of death never bothers me.
I am often distressed by the way time flies so very rapidly.
I fear dying a painful death.
The subject of life after death troubles me greatly.
I am really scared of having a heart attack.
I often think about how short life really is.
I shudder when I hear people talking about a World War III.
The sight of a dead body is horrifying to me.
I feel that the future holds nothing for me to fear.

Source: Templer, D. The construction and validation of a death anxiety scale. *Journal of General Psychology*, 1970, **82**, p. 167. Reprinted by permission.

Only Boyar's (1964) Fear of Death Scale (FODS) and Templer's (1970) Death Anxiety Scale (DAS) have been validated. Validation is a procedure for determining whether a scale measures what it was designed to measure—in this case, death anxiety. Exactly how this should be done varies with the type of scale used. Boyar attempted to validate his scale by administering it to subjects before and after viewing a highway accident movie that was intended to increase their death anxiety. Fear of death scores rose significantly more in the experimental group than in the control group that saw an innocuous movie.

Templer validated his scale both with psychiatric patients in a state mental hospital and with college students. High-anxiety psychiatric patients independently assessed by a clinician were found to have significantly higher DAS scores than control patients.

The remaining four scales (Collett and Lester, 1969; Lester, 1967; Sarnoff and Corwin, 1959; Tolor, 1967) have not been independently validated, although intercorrelations among the scales are high enough to lend each a degree of concurrent validity. Durlak (1972a) found positive intercorrelations ranging from 0.41 to 0.65 among five of the scales. He inexplicably omitted Templer's DAS from his study, although Templer (1970) reported a positive 0.74 correlation between his scale and Boyar's (1964) FODS.

Two remaining scales (Dickstein, 1972, 1975; Kreiger, Epsting, and Leitner, 1974) have neither been validated nor compared to the six scales discussed above. Kreiger, Epsting, and Leitner's (1974) Threat Index has the interesting feature of being theoretically based, but it has poor test-retest reliability ($r=0.49$ with one of 13 subjects dropped). *Test-retest reliability* is a measure of the reliability of the scale over time. That is, if an individual completes the same scale at different times, her or his scores should be very similar even though several months may have passed between the first and second time the scale was administered. This is based on the assumption that the scale measures permanent dispositional characteristics of the individual which should not vary greatly over time.

Most death anxiety scales treat death anxiety as a unitary concept. This is based on the probably erroneous assumption that death anxiety is a single type of fear or anxiety. The one exception is the Collett and Lester (1969) scale, which is divided into four subscales that measure anxiety over death of self, death of others, dying of self, and dying of others. These subscales are roughly equivalent to the fear of nonbeing and the fear of the process (the pain and suffering) of dying as they apply to ourselves and those close to us. Collett and Lester found low intercorrelations among their subscales, especially between the two subscales dealing with self and the two dealing with others, suggesting that death anxiety is a multidimensional concept. An individual may, for example, fear the process of her or his own dying and not be fearful about the dying process of those close to her or him.

Durlak's (1972a) intercorrelation study showed that other scales correlate best with the death-of-self subscale of Collett and Lester. Many of the inconsistencies in the death anxiety data will probably be clarified once researchers begin paying closer attention to the components of death anxiety instead of treating it as a unitary concept. One such attempt is made below in the section on sex differences, where it is argued that inconsistencies in the literature are resolved when the cognitive and affective components of death anxiety are isolated. The accurate assessment of death anxiety is further complicated by recent findings that the method of administering a death anxiety scale affects reported death anxiety.

Schulz, Aderman, and Manko (1976) found significantly lower reported death anxiety among college students on the Templer (1970) and Sarnoff and Corwin (1958) scales when they were administered individually rather than in group sessions. Death anxiety as measured by a group-administered questionnaire was not significantly different from death anxiety as assessed by the *bogus pipeline method* (Jones and Sigall, 1971), in which a fake *emotion monitoring device* is attached to subjects to keep them honest. The rationale underlying the bogus pipeline method is that subjects do not want to be second-guessed by a machine, and when asked to predict what the machine says about their attitudes, they respond without many of the social biases that obscure straight paper-and-pencil measures on sensitive topics. The findings of Schulz et al. suggest that there may be a private and public component to death anxiety and that the private attitudes are more likely to be expressed when the respondent is anonymous.

In addition to the problems of the *unitary concept assumption*, death anxiety scales have been criticized by some researchers for their inability to discriminate between private and "nonconscious" death anxiety. For example, Fulton (1961) has argued that even with a valid and reliable measuring instrument, a researcher can still only tap the "epiphenomenal" or surface-level attitudes of subjects, while Rheingold (1967) has stated that even the most elegant instrument can measure only public attitudes "passively acquired from culture or religion" and completely miss those attitudes and feelings existing at the unconscious level. In order to delve into the unconscious, according to Rheingold, it is necessary to turn to projective techniques and the intuitive insights of the psychotherapist. It is difficult to argue against such an approach except by pointing out its subjective nature.

More objective measurements of nonconscious death anxiety are possible by comparing reaction time, recall reaction time, galvanic skin response for death-related and neutral-word associations, or through use of the Color Word Interference Test (Stroop, 1938). Presumably, these indirect techniques assess death anxiety on a level beneath that accessible by questionnaires, although results from such studies must be interpreted with care.

Researchers have assumed that high galvanic skin response or slow reaction time during death-related word-association tasks indicate *perceptual defense* and, hence, death anxiety (Alexander and Adlerstein, 1958; Feifel and Branscomb, 1973). Using a different indirect technique, Lester and Lester (1970) found that recognition of blurred death-related words was faster than recognition of blurred neutral words. They explained that *perceptual facilitation* makes evolutionary sense, since survival requires hasty recognition of threatening stimuli. Since most investigators of nonconscious death anxiety use word-association rather than word-recognition tasks, the focus of this research has been on processes of perceptual defense rather than perceptual facilitation.

Another indirect technique is analysis of dream content. Handal and Rychlak (1971) had several judges (inter-rater reliability = 0.89) classify dreams reported in subjects' morning-after journals as positive, negative, or neutral, and as death-related or nondeath-related. They considered a high frequency of negative and/or death-related dreams to be evidence of nonconscious death anxiety.

Taken together, these studies indicate that the measurement of death anxiety is indeed a more complex task than early researchers had anticipated. At present, it appears that death anxiety is not a unitary concept and may be comprised of four or more subcomponents. To complicate matters even further, it appears that death anxiety can be tapped at any one of three levels: public, private, and nonconscious. Table 2.2 shows the three levels crossed by possible sub-components. Although it is unlikely that each of 57 possible cells can be clearly differentiated operationally, death anxiety researchers should nevertheless be sensitive to the complexity of their task, if confusion is to be avoided in the future.

Demographic and personality correlates of death anxiety

Though many variables have been found to relate to death anxiety, few clear and consistent patterns have emerged. The search for such patterns in the data is reviewed below.

Sex Although several early studies yielded no systematic sex-related differences in death anxiety (Christ, 1961; Rhudick and Dibner, 1961;

TABLE 2.2   *Specific death fears by different assessment methods.*

	Level of assessment		
	Public	Private	Nonconscious
Specific fears relating to death of self*			
Pain			
Body misfunction			
Humiliation			
Rejection			
Non-being			
Punishment			
Interruption of goals			
Negative impact on survivors			
a) psychological suffering of survivors			
b) economic hardship			

*All these fears can be experienced vicariously in relation to the death of someone close to us. In addition, the fear of abandonment can be experienced directly.

Swenson, 1961; Jeffers, Nichols, and Eisdorfer, 1961), it now appears fairly certain that, on the level assessed by questionnaires, females fear death more than males. Templer's (1970) DAS has been administered to samples of apartment residents, hospital aides, psychiatric patients, ninth graders, and high school students, and their parents (Templer, Ruff, and Franks, 1971; Iammarino, 1975), and in all cases females scored higher than males. This finding was replicated by several other researchers.

Only when death anxiety is broken up into its components do researchers find any evidence of a greater fear of death among males. According to Thematic Apperception Test (TAT) responses, males have more fear of the effects of their death on dependents (Diggory and Rothman, 1961) and more fear of the violence of death (Lowry, 1965). In contrast, women show more fear of the dissolution of the body and the physical pain associated with death (Diggory and Rothman, 1961).

Degner (1974) identified two clusters of responses to the concept of death by having subjects fill out 36 semantic differential scales. Among males, she found an *evaluative dimension* to be strongest and an *emotional dimension* to be weakest. In an earlier study, Folta (in Degner, 1974) found the reverse to be true for females. These studies suggest that there may be a cognitive and emotional component to death anxiety, with females viewing death in more emotional terms and males viewing death in more cognitive terms.

Consistent with these findings is the preliminary work done by Krieger, Epsting, and Leitner (1974) with their Threat Index, a scale that measures death anxiety by measuring the *cognitive distance* subjects place between the concepts "death" and "self." Males tend to have higher death anxiety scores than females—a finding directly contrary to that obtained when Lester's death anxiety scale is used. Since the Threat Index is a cognitive measure and Lester's death anxiety scale is a more affective one, these results and those of Degner and Folta can be understood if it is accepted that male death anxiety tends to be cognitive and female death anxiety tends to be more emotional.

Further support for the existence of these two components of death anxiety is the lack of correlation between Lester's affective death anxiety scale and the more cognitive Threat Index (Krieger, Epsting, and Leitner, 1974) and also the lack of correlation between Lester's death anxiety scale and Boyar's FODS, which is also supposedly a more "cognitive" scale (Krieger, Epsting, and Leitner, 1974; Berman and Hays, 1973). Finally, Krieger et al. reported a very high positive ($+0.73$, $p < 0.01$) correlation between the two cognitive scales—the Threat Index and Boyar's FODS.

Age Although most of the death anxiety data have been collected from college students and the aged, there are some pertinent data available for every age group, from infants to the very old. Hall and Scott (in Hall, 1922) attempted to assess death anxiety in children by asking adults to recall their earliest experiences with death. Using this retrospective technique, they concluded that the young child's view of death is characterized by specific objects and feelings associated with a specific death.

A more informative study on children's death anxiety was conducted by Nagy (1959) who directly interviewed 378 boys and girls, three to ten years old. Nagy's results yielded three relatively discrete developmental phases: (1) for ages three to five, death is seen as a temporary departure or sleep; (2) for ages five to nine, death is seen as final and is personified as either a separate person or the dead person;

and (3) for ages nine and above, death is recognized as not only final, but also inevitable. Nagy's data suggest that the association between death and anxiety is established as early as three years of age, when death is viewed as separation.

According to Rothstein (in Kastenbaum and Aisenberg, 1972), death anxiety is relatively low throughout young adulthood and until the middle adult years. Relying on extensive interview data, he found that death anxiety peaks in the middle years. This is especially true for males, perhaps because this is the first time they become aware of their own vulnerability as a result of deaths among friends and acquaintances their age.

Contrary to Rothstein's findings, Feifel and Branscomb (1973) found that subjects over the age of 50 tended to answer "no" to the question, "Are you afraid of your own death?" more frequently than younger subjects. On the other hand, a study by Templer, Ruff, and Franks (1971) yielded results contrary to both Rothstein, and Feifel and Branscomb. Testing over 2000 subjects of various ages, they found no significant correlation between age and death anxiety scores. This discrepancy in findings remains unresolved and is further complicated by a study of death anxiety at the nonconscious level.

Feifel and Branscomb (1973) found that elderly subjects who reported below-average overt death anxiety exhibited nonconscious death anxiety that was just as high as that of younger subjects. Corey (1961) similarly found that older adults tend to show avoidance of death in projective tests. Perhaps these data can be understood if it is assumed that people are more likely to deny their fears as death becomes a more immediate threat.

Physical health Evidence on the relationship between health and death anxiety follows a pattern similar to that of death anxiety and age. There is conflicting evidence on overt death anxiety and a possibility of denial among those subjects most threatened by impending death. Lucas (1974) studied 60 hemodialysis and surgery patients and did not find their DAS scores to be significantly different from the normal mean scores reported by Templer (1970). Templer, however, found a significant negative correlation between scores on the DAS and a measure of physical health, indicating that the higher an individual's death anxiety the lower her or his physical health status.

Swenson (1961) suggested that people who are unhealthy might look forward to ending it all and so might fear death less than healthy individuals. His finding, that individuals in poor health tended to look forward to death more than fear it, supports this view, although his sample included only aged individuals. Feifel and his colleagues (Feifel, 1974; Feifel, Freilich, and Hermann, 1973) found that terminally ill patients reported fearing death no more frequently than other subjects, but demonstrated higher death anxiety on a nonconscious level.

Kübler-Ross (1969) reports some impressionistic data based on interviews with 200 terminal patients. She found that although patients experienced a great deal of shock and anxiety when first informed of their terminality, most patients eventually came to accept their impending deaths. In a review of the literature on the feelings and attitudes of dying patients, Schulz and Aderman (1974) concluded that the predominant response of most terminal patients is depression rather than anxiety shortly before death.

Religiosity While Lester's review (1967a) reported considerable confusion on the influence of religious belief on death anxiety, recent findings have been refreshingly clear. It is possible that the disparate results from earlier studies (e.g., Faunce and Fulton, 1958; Kalish, 1963) are attributable to different conceptualizations of religiosity. Indicators of extrinsic religiosity (frequency of church attendance) might result in a positive relationship between religiosity and death anxiety, but religiosity measured in terms of fundamental values might produce the reverse relationship. Recent studies show that degree of religiosity (measured by self-reported beliefs and churchgoing) is unrelated to death anxiety for the general population (Feifel, 1974; Kalish, 1963; Templer, 1970), but it is negatively related when subjects are religiously involved (Templer, 1972a; Shearer, 1973)—that is, for Templer's sample, which included many ministers, religiosity was correlated with low levels of death anxiety.

Belief in afterlife has been suggested as an intervening variable reducing death anxiety for highly religious people. Jeffers et al. (1961) found that individuals with strong religious commitments were more likely to believe in afterlife and also showed less fear of death than less religiously committed persons. Osarchuck and Tatz (1973) found that, for subjects scoring high on a Belief in Afterlife Scale, a death-threatening slide show induced still greater belief in an afterlife. In general, the link between belief in afterlife and religiosity has been amply demonstrated. Osarchuck and Tatz (1973) and Kalish (1963) reported that active Protestants and Catholics had higher belief in afterlife when compared to religiously inactive persons of any faith. The other link—the relationship between belief in afterlife and death anxiety, independent of degree of religiosity—is in need of further study.

Emotional disorders Research on the death anxiety of psychiatric patients is inconsistent. Broadman, Erdman, and Wolff (1956) and Templer (1971a) found psychiatric illness positively associated with high death anxiety. Similarly, Templer and Ruff (1971) reported above average DAS means for samples of psychiatric patients. However, contradictory findings are reported by Feifel and Hermann (1973). Using a wide range of death anxiety measurement devices, Feifel and Hermann found no differences between the death anxiety of mentally ill and normal subjects. They also found the degree of mental illness to be unrelated to death anxiety.

Working with samples of "normals" from the general public, Templer (1970, 1972a) reported small positive correlations between Templer's DAS and the neuroticism scales of the Eysenck Personality Inventory and the Welsh Anxiety Scale, respectively. Other scales of general anxiety correlate similarly with the DAS (Templer, 1970; Lucas, 1974), as does the Minnesota Multiphasic Personality Inventory (MMPI) depression scale (Templer, 1971a). Using projective measures, Rhudick and Dibner (1961) found significant positive correlations between death concern and four MMPI scales of neurotic preoccupation. These findings indicate that death anxiety shares features with more general forms of anxiety, neurosis, and depression. While it is important not to ignore this aspect of death anxiety, it is also important to note that Templer (1970) reports data suggesting that death anxiety is a concept distinct from general anxiety. The intercorrelations among various death anxiety scales are consistently and significantly higher than their correlations with general anxiety.

It might be expected that people who attempt suicide would fear death less than the general population. Lester (1967a) found this to be the case when he administered his and Boyar's (1964) FODS to attempters and threateners of suicide and compared their scores to those of subjects who never considered suicide. Similarly, Tarter, Templer, and Perley (1974) found a significant correlation between the DAS and the judged "potential for rescue" following the act of attempted suicide. One possible interpretation of these data is that those who fear death less are more serious about acting on their suicidal desires. The only evidence contrary to these findings comes from an unpublished study carried out by Lester and reported in his review (1967a). He found that suicide-threateners fear death more than suicide-contemplators, who in turn fear death more than those who have never considered taking their lives; Lester admits this evidence is weak because of the small sample studied. The best conclusion is that suicidal individuals have lower death anxiety than comparable nonsuicidal populations.

Need for achievement, sense of competence and purpose At least three hypotheses have been generated relating a need for achievement, a sense of competency, and a sense of purpose in life to death anxiety:

1   Individuals with a high *need for Achievement* (nAch) will fear death more because it ends their chance for further achievement (Diggory and Rothman, 1961).

2   Individuals with a high sense of competence will fear death less because they are satisfied with their lives (Goodman, 1975).

3   Persons with low fear of death will have a greater purpose in life because a crucial step in developing the latter is confronting death without fear (Frankl, 1965).

Two studies (Nogas, Schweitzer, and Grumet, 1974; Ray and Najam, 1974) investigated the first hypothesis and failed to find a relationship between nAch and death anxiety, although Ray and Najam pointed out that the undergraduate samples used were too high in nAch to provide a sufficiently wide range of scores. The second hypothesis was partially supported by Nogas et al. (1974), who found a significant negative correlation between death anxiety and sense of competence. The data may indicate, however, that a sense of competence includes competence in confronting death. The third hypothesis is supported by convincingly high negative correlations (ranging from -0.54 to -0.83) between overt death anxiety and Crumbaugh and Maholick's (1964) Purpose in Life Test (Blazer, 1973; Durlak, 1972b, 1973b). Ignoring the fact that correlations say little about causality or about direction of causality, Blazer and Durlak suggest that children taught to accept death will become adults with more meaning in their lives.

Cognitive style A provocative study by Mishara, Baker, and Kostin (1972) indicated that college students differing in cognitive style hold different attitudes toward death. Cognitive style was determined by the Kinesthetic Figural Aftereffects task, which classifies subjects as *augmenters* if they overestimate the width of a wooden block held between their fingers after holding a wider *intervening stimulus* block. Subjects who underestimate the block's width after the intervening stimulus are classified as *reducers*. Augmenters tend to magnify stimulus intensity; they tend to be more comfortable with stimulus deprivation and less comfortable with *aversive stimuli*. When asked to imagine the final year of their lives, augmenters avoided mentioning death (presumably an aversive stimulus) significantly more than reducers. While no death anxiety scale was administered in this study, these data suggest that augmenters have more death anxiety than reducers.

This attempt to link death anxiety to cognitive functioning is a refreshing change from the usual pattern of relating death anxiety to other questionnaire measures.

Other variables A host of other variables have been researched as possible correlates of death anxiety. No significant correlations were found for the following variables: projective measures of fear of failure (Cohen and Parker, 1974); a dependency scale (Selvey, 1973); guilt about hostility (Selvey, 1973); race (Pandey, 1974; Pandey and Templer, 1972); and Eysenck's Extraversion Scale (Templer, 1972b). Three of four studies relating death anxiety to Rotter's I-E Locus of Control Scale reported no relationship (Selvey, 1973; Dickstein, 1972; Berman, 1973); only Tolor and Reznikoff (1967) found a significant relationship between Rotter's I-E Scale and death anxiety. Externally oriented subjects had significantly greater death anxiety than subjects with internal orientations.

Denial of death anxiety
The idea that death anxiety can exist at both the conscious and nonconscious level has been a theme throughout this chapter. While researchers have occasionally found consistencies between self-reported and nonconscious death anxiety, more often than not the two are discrepant. When such discrepancies occur, researchers typically

invoke the concept of repression or denial of death anxiety to explain these findings. The evidence for such processes is discussed next.

Handal and Rychlak (1971) found a much higher proportion of negative and death-related dreams among subjects who scored high or low on self-report death anxiety scales than among those with moderate scores. They concluded that many of those with low conscious death anxiety were denying their deeper fears. Feifel and his colleagues (Feifel and Branscomb, 1973; Feifel and Hermann, 1973) concluded that death anxiety is greater at nonconscious than at conscious levels, especially for aged and unhealthy subjects. For this reason, the concept of denial has been invoked to explain the lack of increased death anxiety scores among dying subjects. Similarly, the failure to find a relationship between death anxiety and contact with death may be attributed to the exclusive use of conscious death anxiety measures in these studies.

Other evidence of denial of death anxiety makes use of Byrne's (1964) Repression-Sensitization Scale. Subjects who tend to repress threats (according to the Repression-Sensitization Scale) also tend to be low in conscious death anxiety as measured by the DAS (Templer, 1971b). Templer found no evidence for the relationship between the Repression-Sensitization score and nonconscious death anxiety. Apparently repressors, while low in conscious death anxiety, are not high in nonconscious death anxiety either.

Templer (1971b) also found a 0.30 correlation between DAS and nonconscious death anxiety as measured by galvanic skin response to death related stimulus material. This moderately positive correlation suggests that the two levels of death anxiety are not totally independent.

Donaldson (1972) argues that operational and theoretical definitions of denial must be determined before conclusions are drawn about its existence. The discrepancies between conscious and nonconscious death anxiety found in the research reviewed above seem to serve as adequate operational definitions. The next step should be to refrain from further attempts to find correlates of conscious death anxiety and to begin to treat death anxiety as a multilevel concept. Research employing discrepancy between conscious and nonconscious death anxiety as a variable and searching for its correlates appears promising. The internal dynamics resulting from disharmony between different levels of a person's attitudes toward death may prove to be more important than death anxiety itself.

Environmental influences on death anxiety

Three classes of environmental variables are found in the literature. Researchers have examined the effects of educational intervention, contact with death, and the family on death anxiety. Lucas (1974) and Templer, Ruff, and Franks (1971) reported high correlations ($r = 0.59$) between spouses' DAS scores; child-parent correlations were less ($r = 0.40$), but tended to be somewhat higher when the two are of the same sex. Although these data say nothing about the relative importance of environment and genetics as determinants of death anxiety, they do support the notion that the environment, through parents' influence, affects death anxiety (Templer, Ruff, and Franks, 1971).

Lester and Templer (1972) found a striking developmental trend in child-parent correlations. During adolescence, daughter-parent DAS correlations decreased steadily and were statistically insignificant by age 18 or 19. No explanation is offered for the apparent tendency for adolescent boys to continue to be influenced by their parents while their sisters are cutting the death anxiety "apron strings." Another finding of family influence was reported by Iammarino (1975). Ninth graders living with only one parent feared death more than their two-parent peers. This could be interpreted as evidence that separation anxiety can be an antecedent of death anxiety. More generally, this serves to demonstrate the effect of family environment on death anxiety.

Since death anxiety has been shown to be a socially influenced phenomenon, one might expect it to respond to direct intervention. However, attempts to verify the success of intervention, in the form of nursing curricula and college courses, have met with mixed success. Nurses nearing graduation accept death more than students earlier in their training (Yeaworth, Kapp, and Winget, 1974). Their death anxiety is lower (Lester, Getty, and Kneisl, 1974), and thoughts of death are less frequent (Snyder, Gertler, and Ferneau, 1973). With the exception of Lester and his colleagues, most researchers attribute the changes in death anxiety to the nursing curriculum, ignoring alternative explanations such as contact with patients. All that can be concluded with certainty is that something in a nursing student's experience reduces death anxiety.

Several specific *death education programs* have been evaluated, but only one caused a significant reduction in death anxiety. Murray (1974) found that nurses' DAS scores were significantly reduced after a six-week course. It is possible that the practical work of the students interacted with the program to lessen death anxiety, since courses for college students have not changed death anxiety significantly (Bell, 1975; Leviton, 1973; Wittmaier, 1975).

While death education courses will certainly continue in colleges and nursing schools, an indirect approach to lessening death anxiety was shown to be effective by Templer, Ruff, and Simpson (1974). They evaluated the death anxiety of subjects before and after therapy dealing exclusively with reduction of depression. DAS scores declined significantly along with depression, demonstrating that depression and death anxiety covary to some extent.

In spite of many attempts, no study has shown that contact with death or with high-risk stituations influences death anxiety. Self-report of previous death-threatening experiences is unrelated to death anxiety (Durlak, 1973a; Berman, 1974). Nurses' death anxiety is not related to the patient death rate on their unit (Shusterman and Sechrest, 1973) or within their area of specialization (Lester, Getty, and Kneisl, 1974). Parachute jumpers (Alexander and Lester, 1972) and widows (Kalish and Reynolds, 1974; Rhudick and Dibner, 1961) score no higher than controls on death scales, although Swenson (1961) found that widows tend to deny their death anxiety when direct methods are used. These findings again point to the importance of knowing the level at which death anxiety is being assessed.

Future research
This review of the death anxiety literature suggests that future research should move in three directions. First, researchers should be sensitive to the multidimensionality of death anxiety. Much of the confusion of past research may be avoided by recognizing that death anxiety is comprised of several independent components, each of which can be tapped at a public, private, and nonconscious level. An immediate goal should be the investigation of the various sub-components of death anxiety. Some components—such as anxiety over nonexistence and the anxiety over the process of dying (that is, the humiliation, pain, and suffering) in relation to self and others—have been identified. Other components might include anxiety about the impact of one's death on survivors or about having one's plans interrupted.

A second endeavor should be the untangling of discrepancies between conscious and nonconscious death anxiety. The consequences of this discrepancy may eventually prove more interesting and important than simple death anxiety per se. One perspective on this problem is presented in a recent excellent review of the psychological death literature by Kastenbaum and Costa (1977). These authors suggest that fear of death and death anxiety are two different and independent phenomenon. Thus an individual may have strong specific fears associated with death and yet exhibit little death anxiety. Viewed from this perspective, there is no reason to expect a consistent relationship between conscious and nonconscious death anxiety. At any rate, further attempts at enlarging the list of correlates of death anxiety appear to be of little use in understanding or demonstrating its relevance to human behavior.

Third, an effort should be made to demonstrate the functional or behavioral consequences of death anxiety. One such example is Templer's (1972b) study of death anxiety in smokers. Templer found that while nonsmokers and smokers did not differ in death anxiety, smokers with high death anxiety tended to smoke less. Another example is Kastenbaum and Briscoe's (1975) study of street-crossing behavior. The authors demonstrated the feasibility of relating naturalistically observed behavior to unobserved psychosocial variables. They found strong relationships between risk-taking in street-crossing and suicidal tendencies, marital status, and desired and expected life span.

Schulz and Aderman (1977) investigated the relationship between physicians' death anxiety and the length of their patients' survival in the hospital. It was hypothesized that physicians high in death anxiety would be less willing to admit that their patients were terminal and therefore more likely to use heroic measures to keep them alive. Thus, these patients, once admitted to the hospital, should survive longer than the terminal patients of physicians with low death anxiety.

To test this hypothesis, 27 physicians at a southern community hospital were told that the researcher was calling on a variety of professional people as part of an attitude survey and that the survey dealt with attitudes toward death. After explaining that they were to indicate their agreement or disagreement, using a scale from -3 to +3, the following five statements (Sarnoff and Corwin, 1959) were read to each physician:

1   I tend to worry about the death toll when I travel on highways.
2   I find it difficult to face up to the ultimate fact of death.

3 Many people become disturbed at the sight of a new grave, but it does not bother me.

4 I find the preoccupation with death at funerals upsetting.

5 I am disturbed when I think of the shortness of life.

The 27 physicians interviewed were divided into three groups which reflected the degree of death anxiety: (1) high ($n = 8$); (2) medium ($n = 7$); and (3) low ($n = 9$). Their hospital records were examined to determine the number of patients each physician treated, the number that died, and the average length of stay in the hospital of dying patients and nondying patients. The relevant data are presented in Table 2.3.

TABLE 2.3 *Average stay in hospital of dying and non-dying patients and percent of total patients who died by the level of death anxiety of attending physicians.*

	Level of death anxiety of attending physicians		
	High (n=8)	Medium (n=7)	Low (n=9)
Average stay of dying patients* (in days)	14.49	9.98	8.45
Average stay of nondying patients (in days)	11.20	9.76	10.46
Percent of total patients treated who died	3.25	5.32	3.32

*$F(2,22) = 3.52$, $p < 0.05$.

The length of stay for dying patients varied directly as a function of the physicians' death anxiety. Patients of physicians with high death anxiety were in the hospital an average of 14.49 days before dying, while patients treated by physicians of medium and low death anxiety were in the hospital 9.98 and 8.45 days, respectively. One possible interpretation of these data is that physicians with high death anxiety admit terminal patients earlier and/or are more likely to use heroic measures to keep them alive. Table 2.3 also shows that the nondying patients do not differ as to length of stay in the hospital as a function of their physicians' death anxiety. The percent of deaths per group of physicians also does not vary as a function of level of death anxiety. Taken together these data suggest that death anxiety may affect the physicians' policy regarding the treatment of terminal patients. These data are only correlational, and much additional information would be necessary to substantiate this hypothesis.

This experiment represents one way of relating death anxiety to some specific behavioral outcomes. To the extent that death anxiety can be related to and can influence an individual's functioning, the pursuit of this concept should become a useful and important endeavor.

CONCLUSION

Thinking about death has been one of humanity's major preoccupations. Many early speculations were based on intuition and individual case studies, and they yielded a rich and complex perspective on what it is that humanity fears about death and on how these fears affect its functioning. Some researchers (Becker, 1973; Meyer, 1975; Zilboorg, 1943) have used this perspective to argue that death anxiety has been the inspiration for many great individual achievements. Turning to the empirical studies of the relationship between death anxiety and a multitude of other variables, we found this approach to be somewhat simplistic. Death anxiety does not appear to be a unidimensional concept. Instead, it appears to have many components, each of which can be assessed at different levels. However, recent research shows signs of tapping into the richness of this topic. ?

3

THE DEMOGRAPHY OF DEATH

Although humanity has accomplished much during the last three decades, it has not yet found a cure for death. People still die, and they die at predictable rates and of predictable causes. Two significant changes have occurred in the last 100 years, though. First, we live longer now than we did then. Average life expectancies have increased, with infants, children, young adults, and females of all ages showing the largest gains. Second, the major causes of death have changed. Communicable diseases such as tuberculosis, influenza, and pneumonia have been replaced by degenerative diseases such as heart disease, cancer, and strokes as the leading causes of death.

What is meant by *life expectancy*? Life expectancy is defined as the average duration of life. It is the number of years lived by the average person of a group born in a particular year. When we say that the life expectancy in the United States in 1900 was 47.3, we mean that at birth, an individual born in 1900 could, on the average, expect to live 47.3 years. Individuals born in 1971 have an estimated life expectancy of 71 years. This appears to be an amazing increase in longevity; however, it is largely due to reduced deaths at early ages. Since many more individuals born in 1900 died in infancy and early childhood, the average life expectancy was naturally greatly reduced. Thus persons who survived the first decade of life, even if they were born in 1900, could expect to live significantly longer than the average life expectancy.

For example, a 15-year-old individual who was born in 1900 could expect to live to the age of 66; if this same individual lived to be 65, she or he could expect to live 12 more years. A 15-year-old individual who was born in 1971 will likely live to the age of 78, while a 65-year-old individual of this group can, on the average, look forward to another 15 years of life. The difference in predicted longevity for 65-year-old people who were born in either 1900 or in 1971 is only three years. We can conclude from this that, while we are not living much longer than people did 100 years ago, a greater proportion of us are attaining old age.

Reliable documentation for determining life expectancy has only been available for roughly the last century. Scholars have, however, estimated the average duration of life from prehistoric times to the nineteenth century. Dublin (1951), for example, estimated that prehistoric people lived, on the average, about 18 years. This appraisal is consistent with longevity estimates of the few remaining groups in

Africa and elsewhere, whose living conditions resemble those of the prehistoric people.

As Lerner (1976, p. 141) described it,

Life during prehistory was, in the Hobbesian sense, indeed nasty, short, and brutish. Violence was the usual cause of death, judging from the many skulls found with marks of blows, and man's major preoccupation was clearly with satisfying his elemental need for survival in the face of a hostile environment including wild beasts and other men perhaps just as wild. Survivorship in those days was very seldom beyond the age of 40. Persons who reached their mid-20's or more rarely their early 30's, were ipso facto *considered to have demonstrated their wisdom and were, as a result, often treated as sages.*

As civilizations grew and living conditions improved, longevity increased. Lerner (1976) estimates that average life expectancies for people of ancient Greece and Rome were 20 and 22 years, respectively. By the Middle Ages, the life expectancy had probably risen to 33 years. The life expectancy in the Massachusetts Bay Colony of North America was about 35 years. A century later in England and Wales, the life expectancy was 41 years. Data are available for the United States beginning with the year 1900, and life expectancies at several intervals are presented in Table 3.1. The available data show that we have experienced significant increases in the average duration of life in the last 75 years, but this trend appears to be slowing down. The rate of increase for the first 15 years of this century was a little less than six months per year. From 1945 to 1971, the rate of increase had declined to less than a month per year. The leveling off of the death rate can be seen in Fig. 3.1, which shows the steady decline in death rate from 1900 to 1968. Given the present low infant and child mortality rates, it is unlikely that longevity in the United States will increase unless we can prevent or cure heart disease and cancer or reduce the number of accidental deaths.

CAUSE OF DEATH

Causes of death are classified according to criteria established by the World Health Organization and listed in the International Classifica-

TABLE 3.1 *Life expectancies for man from pre-history to contemporary times.*

Time period	Average life span in years
Prehistory	18
Ancient Greece	20
Ancient Rome	22
Middle Ages, England	33
1620 (Massachusetts Bay Colony)	35
19th Century England, Wales	41
1900 USA	47.3
1915 USA	54.5
1954 USA	69.6
1967 USA	70.2
1971 USA	71

Source: Lerner, M. "The demography of death." In E. S. Shneidman (Ed.), *Death: Current perspectives.* Palo Alto, Ca.: Mayfield, 1976, p. 140.

tion of Diseases, Injuries, and Causes of Death, 1955. In addition to classifying diseases, the World Health Organization also specifies the form of the medical death certificate and the coding procedures to be used. Figure 3.2 shows a sample death certificate, which gives the type of information recorded on most death certificates. Note that several causes of death can be indicated. It is the underlying cause of death, however, that is included in the statistical tabulations.

"Diseases of the heart" are the leading causes of death today. (See Table 3.2.) In 1967, 39 percent of all deaths were classified in this category. This represents a significant increase from the 8 percent of deaths attributed to heart disease in 1900. Malignant neoplasms (cancer) and cerebral hemorrhages (strokes—i.e., vascular lesions affecting the central nervous system) are ranked second and third and account for 17 and 11 percent of all deaths, respectively. Again, this represents a major shift in mortality when compared to the causes in the death statistics of 1900. As Table 3.2 indicates, cerebral hemorrhages and malignant neoplasms were ranked fifth and eighth in 1900 and together accounted for only 10 percent of all deaths.

The change in the causes of mortality is graphically demonstrated in Table 3.3, where percent changes in ratio from 1900 to 1970 for four selected causes are presented.

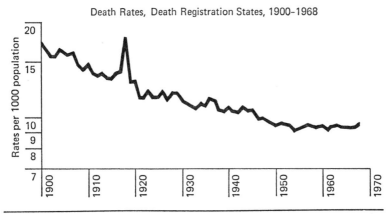

Death Rates, Death Registration States, 1900-1968

FIG. 3.1

*Crude death rate per 1000 population: United States, 1900-1968.
(Source: Reprinted with permission of the publishers. Harvard University Press. From Erhardt, C.L., and Berlin, J.L. (eds.),* Mortality and Morbidity in the United States. *American Public Health Association: Vital & Health Statistics Monographs, 1974, Harvard University Press, courtesy of the National Office of Vital Statistics, U.S. Department of Health, Education, and Welfare.)*

Deaths due to tuberculosis, influenza, and pneumonia decreased by almost 100 percent in 70 years, while deaths due to cardiovascular diseases and cancers increased 43 and 153 percent, respectively, in the same time period. Cardiovascular disease and malignant neoplasms are most common in middle and old age. Therefore, the increase in mortality for these causes is primarily due to more people surviving long enough to be affected by these diseases.

One often overlooked but important cause of death in the United States is accidents. Both in 1900 and 1967 accidents were listed among the ten major causes of death. The increase in the percent of deaths due to accidents (4.2 to 6.1 percent) can be attributed to the increased use and speed of automobiles. The importance of the speed factor is

INDIANA STATE BOARD OF HEALTH
DIVISION OF VITAL RECORDS
MEDICAL CERTIFICATE OF DEATH

Local No._____   State No._____

1. PLACE OF DEATH
a. COUNTY

2. USUAL RESIDENCE (Where deceased lived. If institution Residence before admission)
a. STATE   b. COUNTY

b. CITY, TOWN, OR LOCATION   c. Length of Stay in 1b

c. CITY, TOWN, OR LOCATION

d. NAME OF HOSPITAL OR INSTITUTION (If not in hospital, give street address)

d. STREET ADDRESS

e. IS PLACE OF DEATH INSIDE CITY LIMITS?   YES☐ NO☐

e. IS RESIDENCE INSIDE CITY LIMITS?   YES☐ NO☐

f. IS RESIDENCE ON A FARM?   YES☐ NO☐

3. NAME OF DECEASED (Type or print)   First   Middle   Last

4. DATE OF DEATH   Month   Day   Year

5. SEX

6. COLOR OR RACE

7. MARRIED☐ NEVER MARRIED☐ WIDOWED☐ DIVORCED☐

8. DATE OF BIRTH

9. AGE (In years last birthday)   IF UNDER 1 YEAR Months | Days   IF UNDER 24 HRS. Hours | Min.

10a. USUAL OCCUPATION (Give kind of work done during most of working life, even if retired)   10b. KIND OF BUSINESS OR INDUSTRY

11. BIRTHPLACE (State or foreign country)

12. CITIZEN OF WHAT COUNTRY?

13. FATHER'S NAME

14. MOTHER'S MAIDEN NAME

15. WAS DECEASED EVER IN U. S. ARMED FORCES? (Yes, no, or unknown) (If yes, give war or dates of service)   16. SOCIAL SECURITY NO.

17a. INFORMANT'S NAME

17b. INFORMANT'S ADDRESS

17c. RELATIONSHIP TO DECEASED

18. CAUSE OF DEATH [Enter only one cause per line for (a), (b), and (c).]

PART I. DEATH WAS CAUSED BY:
IMMEDIATE CAUSE (a)_____

Conditions, if any, which gave rise to above cause (a) stating the underlying cause last.   DUE TO (b)_____   DUE TO (c)_____

INTERVAL BETWEEN ONSET AND DEATH

PART II. OTHER SIGNIFICANT CONDITIONS CONTRIBUTING TO DEATH BUT NOT RELATED TO THE TERMINAL DISEASE CONDITION GIVEN IN PART I (a).

19. WAS AUTOPSY PERFORMED?   YES☐ NO☐

20a. ACCIDENT☐ SUICIDE☐ HOMICIDE☐

20b. DESCRIBE HOW INJURY OCCURRED. (Enter nature of injury in Part I or Part II of item 18.)

20c. TIME OF INJURY   Hour a.m. p.m.   Month Day Year

20d. INJURY OCCURRED   WHILE AT WORK☐ NOT WHILE AT WORK☐

20e. PLACE OF INJURY (e. g., in or about home, farm, factory, street, office bldg., etc.)

20f. CITY, TOWN, OR LOCATION   COUNTY   STATE

21. ATTENDING PHYSICIAN: I certify that I attended the deceased from_____ to_____ and last saw him/her alive on_____ M (C.S.T.) on the date stated above; and to the best of my knowledge, from the causes stated.   Death occurred at_____ M (C.S.T.)

22. HEALTH OFFICER: I certify that I investigated cause of death of deceased and find that death occurred at_____ M (C.S.T.) from causes stated and on above date.

23a. Signature of Attending Physician or Health Officer.   23b. ADDRESS   23c. DATE SIGNED

24a. BURIAL, CREMATION, REMOVAL (Specify)   24b. DATE   24c. NAME OF CEMETERY OR CREMATORY   24d. LOCATION

DATE REC'D BY LOCAL HEALTH OFFICER   SIGNATURE OF HEALTH OFFICER   25. FUNERAL DIRECTOR   ADDRESS

S.B.H.—6-24-3—Revised 1955   U. S. Department Health, Education and Welfare.   Form Approved Budget Bureau No. 68-R375

(left margin, vertical) EMBALMER'S NAME   LICENSE No.   MEDICAL CERTIFICATION   FUNERAL DIRECTOR'S LICENSE No.

FIG. 3.2

Sample death certificate. (Source: E. S. Shneidman (ed.), Death: Current Perspectives. Palo Alto, California: Mayfield Publishing, 1976, p. 245.)

illustrated by the reduction of accidental deaths when speed limits were reduced to 55 miles per hour in the 1970s.

Suicide rates vary extensively as a function of age, race, and sex. As Fig. 3.3 indicates, the rate of suicide is highest for white males, especially elderly white males. For nonwhite females and males and for white females, suicide rates generally peak during the early adult and

TABLE 3.2 *The ten leading causes of death:*
United States, 1900 and 1966.

1900

Rank	Cause of death	Rate per 100,000	Percent of all deaths
	All causes	1719.1	100.0
1	Influenza and pneumonia	202.2	11.8
2	Tuberculosis	194.4	11.3
3	Gastroenteritis	142.7	8.3
4	Diseases of heart	137.4	8.0
5	Cerebral hemorrhage	106.9	6.2
6	Chronic nephritis	81.0	4.7
7	Accidents, total	72.3	4.2
8	Malignant neoplasms	64.0	3.7
9	Certain diseases of early infancy	62.6	3.6
10	Diphtheria	40.3	2.3

1966

Rank	Cause of death	Rate per 100,000	Percent of all deaths
	All causes	935.7	100.0
1	Diseases of heart	364.5	39.0
2	Malignant neoplasms	157.2	16.8
3	Cerebral hemorrhage	102.2	10.9
4	Accidents, total	57.2	6.1
5	Influenza and pneumonia	28.8	3.1
6	Certain diseases of early infancy	24.4	2.6
7	General arteriosclerosis	19.0	2.0
8	Diabetes mellitus	17.7	1.9
9	Other diseases of circulatory system	15.1	1.6
10	Other bronchopulmonic diseases	14.8	1.6

Source: National Center for Health Statistics, *Facts of Life and Death*, Public Health
Service Publication No. 600, Washington, 1970, Table 12.

TABLE 3.3   *Selected mortality rates and the percent change in rates: United States, 1900 to 1970.*

Cause of death	Rate per 100,000		Percent change
	1900	1970	
Tuberculosis (all forms)	194.4	2.7	-98.6
Influenza and pneumonia	202.2	30.5	-84.9
Major cardiovascular-renal diseases	345.2	494.0	+43.3
Malignant neoplasms	64.0	162.0	+153.1

Source: Bureau of the Census, *Historical Statistics of the United States, 1900-1957,* Washington, 1958; and Bureau of the Census, *Statistical Abstract of the United States, 1972,* Washington, 1972.

middle years and then decline during old age. Why does the suicide rate for white males increase with age? Several answers to this question are available. In a society largely dominated by white males, white males experience the greatest loss of status with age. They may be more devastated by and fearful of the physical declines associated with aging. They may be more motivated to protect the finances of a surviving wife or children. The most important reason is probably the fact that white males have more to lose as they grow older and are less capable of dealing with these losses.

DEMOGRAPHIC VARIABLES AND DEATH

What is the relationship between socioeconomic status and the death rate? Individuals at the bottom of the socioeconomic ladder—that is, at the poverty level—have the highest death rates. Mortality among the poor is highest during infancy, childhood, and the early adult years. Because they have little access to the personal health services within the private medical-care system, communicable diseases such as influenza and pneumonia are still serious threats to life among poverty groups (Lerner, 1976).

Moving up the socioeconomic ladder, we find that the blue-collar working class has the best overall mortality record. Mortality due to

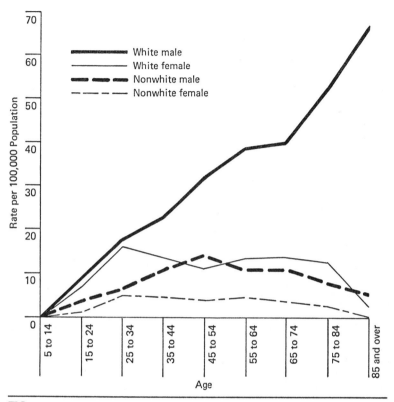

FIG. 3.3

Suicide rates by age and color.
(Source: Vital and Health Statistics,
Series 20, 1967, 5. National Center
for Health Statistics.)

communicable diseases at the younger ages is relatively low because of easy access to good medical care; and, since blue collar workers don't live the sedentary lives of the middle class, they are less likely to contract heart disease caused by obesity, lack of exercise, or the increased occupational stress found among middle-class professionals.

While the higher living standards of the white-collar middle-class professionals is advantageous for longevity during the younger years, it may be a handicap in the later years. During the middle and later years, mortality rates are substantially higher for the white-collar middle-class professionals than for the rest of the population. This is primarily due to the higher incidence of degenerative diseases such as heart disease, cancer, and strokes.

Two explanations have been suggested for the increased mortality of the white-collar middle-class professionals (Lerner, 1976). First, it may be that

because of improved survival by members of this stratum at the younger ages, many persons are carried into mid-life with a lower "general resistance" factor than that which characterizes persons in the poverty stratum, and that these individuals are perhaps therefore more vulnerable to the diseases and hazards most prevalent at mid-life and beyond.

The second possible explanation is that the increased mortality in middle age is a consequence of the life styles of the middle class. Sedentary occupations, which may result in obesity and excessive occupational stresses, and increased smoking contribute to coronary artery disease and respiratory cancer. These characteristics apply primarily to middle-class males. Females in this stratum appear to have the best of both worlds—i.e., they don't experience the health disabilities associated with the stressful sedentary occupations of their spouses and at the same time they have access to good medical care. Of all segments of the population, middle-class females enjoy the greatest longevity and the lowest mortality rates. These statistics may change, however, as more and more women enter the labor force and expose themselves to the occupational stresses that men now experience.

With the exception of deaths caused by cancer of the breast and genital organs, females have lower mortality rates than males for all other causes, regardless of marital status. Table 3.4(a) shows the expected death rates of females and males, classified by marital status and cause of death. Death rates of white married males were used as a standard to compute the expected rates for the other groups. In almost all cases, females outlive males; the only exception is deaths due to cancer of the genital organs. Married females have the lowest death rate, followed by single, widowed, and divorced females. The pattern is identical for males. The same breakdown for non-white persons is presented in Table 3.4(b). Being married is as advantageous for nonwhites as it is for whites. The death rates for married nonwhites, both male and female, are lower than for their single, widowed, or divorced counterparts.

There are many reasons why married individuals live longer; Chapter 5 discusses this matter in greater detail. Briefly, it is likely that married individuals enjoy a higher standard of living, better health care, and receive better nutrition. Selection is also probably important—the more healthy and biologically stronger individuals are more likely to marry.

Comparing Table 3.4(a) with Table 3.4(b) highlights some important differences between whites and nonwhites. The most significant difference is that, as a whole, death rates are higher for nonwhites than for whites of both sexes. A closer examination reveals other interesting differences. Deaths due to coronary disease and suicide are significantly less for nonwhite males than for white males. On the other hand, homicide deaths are ten times higher for nonwhites. The pattern is similar for females.

DEATH RATES: INTERNATIONAL COMPARISONS

The United States does not have the lowest mortality rate in the world. Numerous smaller countries have slightly lower rates, while most countries have rates significantly higher than those of the United States. The death rate per 1000 population for the entire world is 14; for the United States it is 9. A partial listing of death rates for several countries is presented in Table 3.5. As expected, the death rate is high in underdeveloped countries and low in developed countries.

PLACE OF DEATH

Data on where death occurs in the United States have been largely neglected, even though this information can be readily obtained from death certificates. The most recent national data on place of death date back to 1958, but projections for years prior to 1958 can be made from available local data. Table 3.6 shows that the trend has been toward an increased number of deaths in institutions. In 1949, approximately 50 percent of all deaths occurred in hospitals. By 1958, this figure had increased to 61 percent, with the large majority of deaths occurring in general hospitals. Data collected for New York City suggest that this trend is continuing. The percent of deaths in institutions increased

TABLE 3.4(a) Observed death rates per 100,000 population and ratios of expected* to standard death rates of white persons 15 years of age and older by sex and marital status for specified causes of death: United States, 1959-61.

| Cause | Observed rate | | Ratios by marital status | | | | | | | |
| | | | Single | | Married | | Widowed | | Divorced | |
	Male	Female	Male	Female	Male	Female	Male	Female	Male	Female
All causes	1461.8	1041.5	1.52	0.72	1.00	0.59	1.69	0.78	2.24	0.82
Malignant neoplasm of digestive organs and peritoneum	83.6	66.8	1.27	0.79	1.00	0.70	1.32	0.82	1.54	0.79
Vascular lesions affecting central nervous system	148.2	155.2	1.39	0.91	1.00	0.82	1.46	1.02	1.79	1.07
Arteriosclerotic heart disease, including coronary disease	531.2	302.1	1.31	0.45	1.00	0.41	1.40	0.54	1.76	0.52
Cirrhosis of liver	22.3	10.4	2.65	0.48	1.00	0.56	3.97	1.12	6.26	1.47
Malignant neoplasm of genital organs	25.1	35.2	0.95	1.76	1.00	1.51	1.12	1.99	1.36	2.42
Motor vehicle traffic accidents	41.1	13.1	1.69	0.33	1.00	0.37	3.76	0.97	3.88	0.86
Homicide	4.8	1.8	2.05	0.26	1.00	0.43	3.47	1.35	7.23	1.99
Suicide	25.4	7.4	1.94	0.42	1.00	0.31	4.30	0.63	4.18	1.01

*Age distribution of white married men used as a standard to compute expected rates, except for malignant neoplasm of breast for which the age distribution of white married women was used.

Source: National Center for Health Statistics, Division of Vital Statistics, unpublished tables.

TABLE 3.4(b) Observed death rates per 100,000 population and ratios of expected* to standard death rates of black persons 15 years of age and older by sex and marital status for specified causes of death: United States, 1959-61.

Cause	Observed rate		Ratios by marital status							
			Single		Married		Widowed		Divorced	
	Male	Female	Male	Female	Male	Female	Male	Female	Male	Female
All causes	1515.5	1114.1	1.90	1.15	1.18	0.82	2.54	1.46	2.41	1.10
Malignant neoplasm of digestive organs and peritoneum	85.2	51.5	1.66	0.82	1.22	0.66	2.12	1.04	2.16	0.94
Vascular lesions affecting central nervous system	187.4	189.0	2.07	1.78	1.65	1.45	3.16	2.60	2.69	1.73
Arteriosclerotic heart disease, including coronary disease	309.3	203.8	2.11	0.52	0.66	0.38	1.29	0.68	1.14	0.51
Cirrhosis of liver	20.3	12.6	3.04	1.34	0.94	0.65	2.98	1.53	4.01	1.49
Malignant neoplasm of genital organs	31.5	47.1	1.50	2.96	1.61	2.24	2.48	3.79	2.44	3.45
Motor vehicle traffic accidents	48.6	12.2	2.21	0.44	1.25	0.35	2.97	0.71	3.02	0.59
Homicide	54.1	13.7	21.14	4.17	10.41	3.07	37.26	6.41	33.68	5.80
Suicide	12.2	3.0	0.91	0.11	0.46	0.11	1.77	0.28	1.15	0.22

* Age distribution of black married men used as standard to compute expected rates, except for malignant neoplasm of breast for which the age distribution of black married women was used.

Source: National Center for Health Statistics, Division of Vital Statistics, unpublished tables.

TABLE 3.5 *Death rates per 1000: Selected areas and countries of the world, 1976.*

Areas	Death rate
Africa	21
Asia	15
Europe	10
Latin America	10
North America	8
Oceania	10
World	14
Country	
Angola	30
Canada	7
Chile	9
China	9
Cuba	6
France	10
Hong Kong	5
Israel	7
Kenya	18
Kuwait	7
Mexico	8
Netherlands	8
Poland	8
Romania	9
Saudi Arabia	23
Singapore	5
Sweden	11
United States	9
U.S.S.R.	9

Source: United Nations, Population and Vital Statistics Report, Statistical Papers, Series A, Volume XXVIII, November 1, January 1976.

steadily from 66 percent in 1955 to 73 percent in 1967. Deaths occurring at home show a corresponding decrease over time from 31 percent in 1955 to 24 percent in 1967.

TABLE 3.6   *Number and percent of deaths occurring in institutions by type of service of institution, United States, 1949 and 1958.*

	1958		1949	
	Number	Percent	Number	Percent
Total deaths	1,647,886	100.0	1,443,607	100.0
Not in institution	644,548	39.1	728,797	50.5
In institution	1,003,338	60.9	714,810	49.5
Type of service of institution				
General hospital	784,360	46.6	569,867	39.5
Maternity hospital	1,862	0.1	2,249	0.2
Tuberculosis hospital	9,097	0.6	13,627	0.9
Chronic disease, convalescent and other special hospitals	24,180	1.5	12,402	0.9
Nervous and mental hospitals	57,675	3.5	45,637	3.2
Convalescent and nursing homes, homes for the aged, etc.	98,444	6.0	22,783	1.6
Hospital department of institutions, and other domiciliary institutions	3,646	0.2	41,841	2.9
Type of service not specified	24,074	1.5	6,404	0.4

Source: Lerner, M. "The demography of death." In E. S. Shneidman (Ed.), *Death: Current perspectives.* Palo Alto, Ca.: Mayfield, 1976, p. 140.

The increased institutionalization of death has at least two important consequences. First, it means that the medical staff becomes a more significant part of the dying person's life, since these are the people he or she is likely to interact with most frequently before death. A patient may, for example, come to rely on the medical staff for both social and emotional support in addition to medical care. This is likely to cause problems for both the medical staff and the patient, and these problems will be examined in detail later when we discuss medical staff interactions with dying patients.

A second consequence of increased institutionalized deaths is that death becomes removed from our everyday lives. Some persons feel that our present day avoidance of death and death-related topics is largely attributable to the removal of death from the home. It used to be that exposure to death was a natural and common seasoning experience and thought to be essential for a mature and anxiety-free outlook on life. This view has some intuitive appeal, but it is impossible to determine its validity given the available data.

4

THE TERMINAL
PHASE OF LIFE

An ever-increasing number of people must face the prospect of a prolonged period of dying in a hospital or other institution. Already over two-thirds of all deaths occur in hospitals, nursing homes, or similar institutions. But perhaps most distressing of all is the fact that deaths—especially among the aged, who constitute over 80 percent of all who die—are more often than not the result of a prolonged chronic disease such as cancer rather than a quickly terminating acute illness such as pneumonia (Nash, 1975). A consequence of this is that patients, health-care practitioners, and family members must learn to deal with the often lengthy terminal phase of an individual's life.

The terminal phase of life begins when a person with a chronic disease is given the prognosis of steady and rapid deterioration with death expected within a specific period. This deterioration is different from normal aging and is associated with sudden, sharp declines in scores on mental and psychomotor tests, which suggest deterioration of the central nervous system. A terminal prognosis means that there is no reasonable hope of the patient recovering. A person may have a terminal illness (such as cancer), which will eventually kill him, but the disease may be latent or go into remission once manifested. Only the last decline, from which there will be no major remission, is considered the terminal phase.

Physicians do not make terminal prognoses lightly. The decision evolves slowly after many tests of the diagnosis and all available treatments have been tried. Under some circumstances a physician may accept a diagnosis of which he or she is not completely sure rather than put the patient through further tests that are painful or exhaustive. Occasionally, a physician will conclude from the patient's general condition that she or he is dying. There are no universal criteria for terminality, but gross mistakes are rare. The physician must weigh the value of unpredictable possibilities: that patients occasionally show amazing powers of recovery; that further treatment may give a temporary but valuable improvement; that there have been rare cases of spontaneous recovery; and that a new and effective treatment may appear. Usually, the problem in giving a terminal prognosis is not in being proved wrong later, but in deciding how far to pursue treatment when the patient seems to be dying and the diagnosis is uncertain (Hinton, 1967).

It is important that persons caring for the patient know whether recovery is likely. The terminal prognosis implies a shift in the treatment strategy from doing everything possible to initiate a recovery to managing the patient's last days. Another decision that must be made is whether the focus of treatment should be on alleviating discomfort or prolonging life, because all too often these objectives are incompatible. A drug that is useful in alleviating discomfort, morphine, for example, may also shorten the patient's life.

How such conflicts are resolved has implications not only for the patient but also for all individuals interacting with the patient. In the following section, we will examine the profound social and psychological consequences of terminality to the patients, his or her family, and those in charge of his or her care. Three aspects of the terminal phase of life are examined. First, interactions between the medical staff and the dying patient are examined with particular attention paid to the flow of information between practitioners and patients. Second, we will examine the emotional trajectory of the terminal patient and pay close attention to the emotional stages a patient goes through as she or he approaches death. Specific needs of the dying patient and ways in which these needs can be met are discussed in the final section.

THE MEDICAL STAFF AND THE DYING: INFORMING THE PATIENT

In this section, we will examine the attitudes and behaviors which typically characterize the interaction between medical practitioners and the dying patient. The focus will not only be on how doctors and nurses regard death and the dying, but also on the dying patient's feelings regarding her or his condition and the treatment received. The aim is to achieve some understanding of the plight of the dying patient, to learn why he or she is informed or not informed of his or her condition, and to determine how he or she is treated by the medical staff.

Attitudes and behaviors of physicians

Numerous researchers have observed that physicians avoid patients once they begin to die (Livingston and Zimet, 1965; Kubler-Ross, 1969; Glaser and Strauss, 1965; Kastenbaum and Aisenberg, 1972). To explain this avoidance behavior, researchers have focused either on the physicians' training or on their personalities. Those investigators who believe that a basic personality structure is responsible for physicians' behavior toward the dying speculate that some individuals become physicians because of their inordinate fear of death. Becoming a physician, then, has been interpreted as an attempt to master death (Wahl, 1962; Feifel and Heller, 1960; Feifel, Hanson, Jones, and Edwards, 1967). Kasper (in Livingston and Zimet, 1965) agreed with this point of view, adding that . . .

part of the psychological motivation of the physician is to cure himself and live forever; he wished to be a scientist in order to gain mastery over life by treating people as things.

Although not conclusive, some empirical support for self-selection on the basis of personality is found in a study of medical students by Livingston and Zimet (1965). These investigators reasoned that medical students high in authoritarianism—that is, persons who are politically conservative, show latent hostility toward parents, tend not to be introspective, and tend to repress feelings—would be "better defended" against unconscious fears and therefore have less overt death anxiety. As a result, these students would function comfortably in specialities where death is relatively common, for example, surgery. Students low on authoritarianism, on the other hand, would be aware of and made uncomfortable by their death anxiety and as a result choose specialities where death is an uncommon occurrence, for example, psychiatry.

The results supported their hypothesis—i.e., psychiatrically oriented students were less authoritarian and showed higher death anxiety than students oriented toward surgery. The fact that this was true regardless of year of training seems to indicate that medical students decide on a specialty upon entering medical school and this decision is partly determined by their personality structure. Many other variables (intelligence, for example) could explain this relationship; we must therefore be cautious in drawing conclusions from these data.

These personality structures are undoubtedly reinforced by medical training, which emphasizes an interaction style between physician and patient described by Lief and Fox (1963) as *detached concern*. The medical student is advised to be empathetic and involved with the patient but, above all, to remain objective. In addition, the specifics of medical training are usually focused on saving lives to the exclusion of dealing with patients who are defined as terminal. As a consequence both of their personality structures and of the training they receive, physicians may associate dying patients with failure and disappointment. A patient's death challenges the physician's ability as a healer and sensitizes the physician to the temporal limits of her or his own life. It is not surprising then that physicians may tend to avoid patients who are in the process of dying.

Perhaps the most important decision the physician makes when his or her patient becomes terminal is whether or not to tell the patient about his or her condition. There already exists a large body of literature advising the physician on this question (Kubler-Ross, 1969; Glaser and Strauss, 1965; Noyes, 1971; Wahl, 1969; Oken, 1961; Lasagna, 1969; Lirette, Palmer Ibarra, Kroenig, and Gaines, 1969; David, 1971), but only a few researchers have actually tried to determine the extent to which this advice is followed (Oken, 1961; Fitts and Ravdin, 1953).

In an editorial directed at physicians, Lasagna (1969) advised physicians not to lie to the terminal patient about her or his condition. He also recommended that relatives of the patient should be forewarned. Lirette et al. (1969) similarly advised letting patients know their condition, but cautioned physicians to tell the patients gradually. Noyes (1971) pointed out that the physician holds the key to providing the patient with a good death, and that this is best accomplished by informing the patient of his or her condition.

Kübler-Ross (1969) focused on the requirements of a *good death* and stressed the physician's role in fulfilling these requirements. Through intimate interaction, she argued, the physician can help the patient to reach a calm acceptance of her or his death. Wahl (1969) agreed with Kübler-Ross, that the physician should acquire intimate knowledge of the patient, but at the same time he cautioned the physician to be selective in choosing which patients are to be informed of their condition. Although not telling a patient of his or her condition may deprive him or her of the opportunity for sympathetic communication with physicians and friends, there are some individuals who are too afraid of death to face such information. Those patients who are told, Wahl (1969) stresses, should never be told in such a way as to rob them of all hope:

The patient should never be left with the feeling that the physician has played his last card and that nothing further can be done.

Evidence supporting the conclusion that patients shoud be told their condition was reported by Glaser and Strauss (1965). After several years of observing patients and medical staff, they found that most patients learned of their condition from cues given by medical personnel, even when they were not specifically told their condition. These cues ranged in subtlety from facial expressions and avoidance behavior to discussions of the patient's condition in front of the patient.

A number of practitioners have specifically addressed the question of whether or not to tell terminal cancer patients of their condition (Litin, 1960; Hoerr, 1963; Desjardins, 1960; Wyrsch, 1962; Oken, 1961; Schoenberg, Carr, Perety and Kutscher, 1972). Here again, the consensus is that it is best to be truthful, but gentle. Litin (1960) argued that it is a patient's legal right to know the truth. In Hoerr's (1963) opinion, honesty is always the best policy in the long run. Desjardins (1960), Wyrsch (1962), and Oken (1961) all advocated a "play it by ear" policy. In most cases a patient should be told, they advised, but the physician should let the patient be the guide as to how much and in what way the information is conveyed.

Note that most of the advice comes from medical practitioners, primarily doctors, and is therefore directed at colleagues. One would expect that medical doctors might accept such advice, but evidence on the behavior of physicians indicates that this is not the case. Fitts and Ravdin (1953) found that of 442 physicians sampled in a mail survey conducted in the Philadelphia area, over two-thirds of the physicians reported that they infrequently or never disclosed the diagnosis of terminal cancer. A similar nationwide mail survey of over 4000 physicians (Rennick, 1960) revealed that 22 percent never informed patients, while 62 percent sometimes informed patients of incurable cancer.

In a recent study reported by Caldwell and Mishara (1972), 73 medical doctors at a large, private hospital in Detroit were asked to participate in a research project on the attitudes and feelings of medical doctors. Although the majority of physicians consented to participate when first approached, 60 of the 73 doctors refused to complete the interview once they found that the questions dealt with their attitudes toward dying patients. All of the 13 doctors who completed the interview agreed that the dying patient has the right to know that his or her diagnosis is terminal, but only two of those 13 admitted to actually telling their patients of a terminal diagnosis. This inconsistency between attitude and behavior may reflect the fact that physicians find the task of actually informing the patient psychologically too difficult for them and/or not their responsibility.

In a more comprehensive study, Oken (1961) examined not only physicians' behavior as to informing cancer patients, but also what reasons they gave for their behavior. Oken sent a questionnaire to 219 members of the medical staff of Michael Reese Hospital, a private non-profit teaching hospital in Chicago. Ninety-five percent of the questionnaires were returned and 30 percent of those cooperating were subsequently interviewed. Consistent with previous findings, about 90 percent of Oken's respondents indicated that they did not inform patients of their diagnosis; those that did used euphemisms for incurable cancer such as "growth," "hyperplastic tissue," "lesion," "mass," or "tumor."

The primary reason offered for telling those few patients who were told was concern for the patient's financial responsibility. That is, physicians thought it important for some patients to have the opportunity for planning their financial affairs. Primarily emotional reasons were given for not telling the patient: "Knowledge of cancer is a death sentence, a Buchenwald, a torture"; "the cruelest thing in the world"; "like hitting the patient with a baseball bat."

Oken attempted to find out where physicians acquired their policies of not informing patients. Only 5 percent mentioned medical school or hospital training as the major source, whereas the great majority (77 percent) listed clinical experience. Oken reasoned that if experience did indeed determine the physician's policy, then younger doctors should have listed experience less frequently as a determinant of their policy; however, younger doctors were just as likely as older doctors to list experience as a determining factor. Oken concluded that the physicians' claim that their policy is based on experience was far from accurate. Further probing showed that more often than not a physician's policy was based on "opinion, belief, and conviction, heavily weighted with emotional justification" (Oken, 1961) and not on critical observation.

Oken's respondents also voiced substantial opposition to changing their policy on informing patients. Eighty percent felt that policy change in the future was unlikely, although over half felt that they could be swayed by research. A sizable minority stated that they "wouldn't believe it" or "it couldn't be true" if research suggested a policy different from their own. Ten percent of the group objected even to research being carried out in this area.

Attitudes and behaviors of nurses

Although the literature on medical staff other than physicians is sparse, there are some data available on the behavior of nurses toward the dying. A study similar to Oken's was carried out by Pearlman, Stotsky, and Dominick (1969). These investigators interviewed 68 nurses in a variety of institutions—from state hospitals to nursing homes—and found that those nurses having more experience with death were more likely to avoid the dying and felt more uneasy discussing death with dying patients than less experienced nurses.

Lawrence LeShan, reported by Kastenbaum and Aisenberg (1972), measured nurses' avoidance of terminal patients. Using a stop watch, LeShan measured how long it took nurses to respond to bedside calls and found that it took them significantly more time to respond to terminal patients than to less severely ill patients. Apparently, experienced nurses had learned to cope with death by avoiding or denying it, a behavioral pattern similar to that of physicians. Like the physicians in Oken's study, the experienced nurses also advocated experience with dying patients as the best means for learning how to deal with them. The less experienced nurses on the other hand, stressed the need for courses and seminars on managing the dying patient as the best means for learning how to deal with death.

What do nurses tell a patient when directly confronted by her or his thoughts on death? Kastenbaum and Aisenberg (1972) tried to answer this question by asking 200 attendants and nurses at a geriatric hospital how they responded to patients' statements about death (e.g., "I think I'm going to die soon," or "I wish I could just end it all"). Kastenbaum found the following five general categories of responses:

1 *Reassurance:* "You're doing so well now. You don't have to feel this way."

2 *Denial:* "You don't really mean that. . . You're not going to die. Oh, you're going to live to be a hundred."

3 *Changing the subject:* "Let's think of something more cheerful. You shouldn't say things like that; there are better things to talk about."

4   *Fatalism:* "We are all going to die sometime, and it's a good thing we don't know when. When God wants you, He will take you."

5   *Discussion:* "What makes you feel that way today? Is it something that happened, something somebody said?"

The most popular response was some form of avoidance, either fatalism, denial, or changing the subject. The majority (82 percent) evaded any discussion of the patient's thoughts or feelings. "The clear tendency was to *turn off* the patient as quickly and deftly as possible."

Two reasons were given for this behavior. First, the nurses wanted the patient to feel less depressed and they felt that the best way to do this was to get the patient thinking about something else. Second, the nurses wanted to protect themselves—most admitted feeling very uncomfortable talking about death, saying that it "bugged" them or "shook them up" to talk about it.

The inability of nurses to deal with the dying patient is also documented in Jeanne C. Quint's book, *The Nurse and the Dying Patient* (1967). She analyzed nurses' training that could bring about this avoidance behavior and concluded that because young nurses are made to feel very concerned about making mistakes they learn to defend themselves by concentrating on routines and rituals even though these things tend to alienate them from the patients they are caring for. The solution, of course, is to provide professional training early in the nurse's career that will enable him or her to adequately handle the dying patient. Charlotte Epstein has written a book called *Nursing the Dying Patient*, which is aimed at increasing nurses' effectiveness in treating patients who are dying.

It should be apparent now that there is a great disparity between the advice on treatment of terminal patients offered by some practitioners and the behavior of most physicians and nurses. The next section examines the terminal patient's feeling about how he or she is treated by the medical staff and the consequences of such treatment for his or her psychological well-being.

Patients' desire for information about their condition

Kübler-Ross (1969) and Glaser and Strauss (1965) argue that terminal patients acquire information about their condition even if they are not directly informed. The data presented below tend to refute this. Many terminal patients appear to remain unaware of their condition until the end, although it is sometimes difficult to separate what the patient knows from what she or he is willing to accept. Most patients are probably best classified as being in a condition of *uncertain certainty* that Avery Weisman has called *middle knowledge* (Kastenbaum and Aisenberg, 1972). That is, dying patients are aware at some level that they will not recover, but they vacillate between knowing and not knowing this.

Although few researchers have attempted to specifically determine how aware dying patients are of their condition, research on patients' attitudes toward the medical staff and the treatment they receive is more abundant. In his study of healthy nonpatients, psychiatric patients, physically ill patients, and the dying, Cappon (1969) asked each group whether or not they would like to know if a serious illness was terminal. The majority of subjects, regardless of medical status, responded yes. Of the four groups, however, dying patients desired this information least (67 percent). Eighty-one percent of the somatic patients desired such information, while 82 percent of the psychiatric patients and 91 percent of the nonpatients said they would like to know if a serious illness was terminal. Dying patients were also less interested than the other groups in information revealing "when they would die" and "how they would feel on dying."

Cappon concluded from his findings that physicians should be cautious and not give more information than the patient wants. Apparently unaware of the literature showing that physicians only rarely inform patients of their condition, he advised that physicians, as nonpatients, should recognize that "what they *now* think they themselves would want to know may not hold later when they become ill."

Unfortunately, Cappon did not report data on whether or not the dying patients knew their condition was terminal when they filled out his questionnaire. One might expect different attitudes toward death and varying desires for information as a function of such knowledge. It could be that Cappon's dying patients were less curious about *what it's like to die* because they already knew.

Hinton's (1963) work in part addresses itself to this issue. Hinton and his collaborators repeatedly interviewed two groups of patients who resided in the same hospital. One group of 121 patients had fatal illnesses, with death expected within six months; a second group consisted of matched controls who were not dying. These patients entered the hospital at the same time, were the same age, had an illness affecting the same system, and were under the same physician's care. A control patient was always interviewed on the same day as the dying patient. The structure of the interview was left open to the interviewer, provided he or she collected information on age, sex, marital status, social class, strength of religiosity, level of physical distress, depression, anxiety, and the patient's awareness of dying. Since control patients did not differ from dying patients on any of the demographic variables (e.g., sex, age, social class, etc.), Hinton attributed the differences on the psychological variables to degree of illness. Dying patients were significantly more depressed and anxious and were, of course, much more likely to perceive themselves as terminal than non-dying patients.

Looking at relationships between dependent measures, Hinton found that awareness of the possibility of death was significantly related to a mood of depression. Over 60 percent of the dying patients who showed awareness of death expressed mild or moderate depression. These same individuals were not significantly more anxious, although the results were in that direction. Awareness of death was also related to greater physical distress and longer illness.

Depression and anxiety were both related to religious faith, but not in the same way. Those with strong religious beliefs showed the least amount of anxiety but the most depression, while individuals with no religious faith were the least depressed and only slightly more anxious than individuals with strong faith. Patients with some Christian beliefs were high on both anxiety and depression. Perhaps these patients were anxious about their lack of faith and at the same time depressed in the realization that religion really had little to offer. Hinton was unable to offer an explanation for these results or for most of his other findings.

Both Hinton and Cappon concluded that the dying patient is better off not to be informed of her or his condition. Thirty-three percent of Cappon's dying subjects expressed a desire not to be told, while Hinton showed that dying patients who were aware of their condition were more depressed and slightly more anxious than nondying patients. Neither study is, however, convincing in its conclusion. Cappon, for instance, based his conclusion on the fact that fewer dying patients than nondying patients desired information about terminal illness, yet well over half (67 percent) still wanted to know. In addition, Cappon did not report whether these responses came from dying patients who already knew they were dying or from patients who perhaps only suspected it and were afraid to find out. In any case, the conclusion that dying patients more often than not desire information about their condition is better justified by the data than the conclusion offered by Cappon.

Hinton can be criticized on similar grounds. He assumed a causal relationship between awareness of condition and depression. His basic argument was that knowledge of condition leads to depression, which is undesirable; therefore, patients should not be informed. His data also showed that depression was significantly higher in those patients who had endured longer illnesses and greater physical distress. Furthermore, as was indicated earlier, those who had greater physical distress and longer illnesses were more aware of dying. Thus, awareness, depression, physical distress, and longer illness were all positively related in dying patients.

Given these relationships one can just as logically argue that physical distress or longer illness result in depression and awareness of dying; or, perhaps even that depression results in longer illness, greater physical distress, and awareness of dying. Many reasonable causal chains are possible and none can be definitively ruled out given the data presented in this study. Fortunately, other data on this issue are available.

Kelly and Friesen (1950) found that 89 out of 100 cancer patients favored knowing their diagnosis. One hundred clinic patients who did not have cancer were asked if they would like to know the results of an examination that revealed cancer, and the great majority (82 percent) said yes. Similar results are reported by Samp and Curerri (1957), who surveyed 560 cancer patients and their families and found that 87 percent felt that a patient should be told. Subjects who had cancer in these studies were aware of their diagnosis before these surveys were taken. These results are therefore slightly suspect since "patients cannot permit doubts about the wisdom of the policy of those whom they need to trust so desperately" (Oken, 1961).

In a recent interview study, Achte and Vauhkonen (1971), two Finnish psychiatrists, focused on how 100 cancer patients acquired the information that they had terminal cancer. Forty of the patients had been spontaneously told of their condition. Twenty-nine had asked for a diagnosis and received a frank answer, and 31 were reluctant to find out anything about their condition, although six of these patients suspected it was cancer. The majority of the patients (85 percent) had suffered from intense anxiety and depression upon learning the true nature of their illness, but in most cases these symptoms dissipated in a short time.

None of the patients who were spontaneously informed were critical of the act of informing, but a small number did criticize the manner in which they were told, describing the physicians' behavior as tactless and insensitive. Patients who had inquired about their diagnosis were more favorable toward physicians. The remaining patients avoided all discussion of the disease with the interviewer.

This study then lends support to the position that the majority of patients desire to be told and suffer no long-term negative consequences as a result of being informed of their condition. Note, however, that subjects who were informed were not randomly selected: this self-selection may have attenuated the potential negative effects of informing individuals of their condition. The crucial study, where subjects are randomly assigned to information or no information conditions, has not been carried out. The dependent measures in such a study might include an assessment of the psychological and physical well-being of the patient by someone who does not know to which condition a patient was assigned.

THE EMOTIONAL TRAJECTORY OF THE DYING

So far, we have discussed patients' desire for knowledge about their condition, but we have said little about the emotions such knowledge evokes. We will now examine the emotional trajectory (Glaser and Strauss, 1965) of the dying patient and attempt to understand what feelings characterize the terminal phase of life.

Patients' emotional states as well as their attitudes toward death tend to vary as a function of their temporal location in the terminal process. Some authors feel that predictable attitudes emerge in a *stages-of-death model* while others feel that the process is less rigid or even stageless. Probably the strongest and most popular advocate of a *stage theory* of dying has been Elizabeth Kübler-Ross (1969). In *On Death and Dying*, Kübler-Ross outlined a five-stage process of dying based on her observations of 200 patients, of which 197 she believes completed the process prior to death.

According to Kübler-Ross, the patient's initial response to learning that she or he is terminal is shock and numbness. This state is gradually replaced by the first distinct stage in the dying process—*denial*. The patient's reaction at this stage is, "No, not me; it cannot be true." Thus a patient who is convinced that her or his X-rays or lab reports were mixed up with someone else's would be classified in the denial stage. Kübler-Ross argued that this stage is adaptive in that it "acts as a buffer after the unexpected shocking news, allows the patient to collect himself and, with time, mobilize other, less radical defenses."

Denial is followed by *anger*. Patients at this second stage are angry because their plans and activities have been interrupted, and they envy those who can still enjoy life. Frequently, the patient asks, "Why me? Why couldn't it have been somebody else?" From the staff and the family's point of view, this stage is more troublesome than the previous stage since the patient's anger is directed almost randomly at anyone in his or her environment. Kübler-Ross stressed that staff and family must avoid responding personally to anger directed at them.

Bargaining, the third stage in the model, is relatively short. Having been angry at people, and God, in the previous stage, the patient now believes that she or he "can succeed in entering some sort of agreement which may postpone the inevitable happening." Usually the patient offers good behavior (e.g., fervent prayer) in exchange for a postponement of death, but once a specific deadline is reached the patient begins bargaining all over again, asking for more time. Kübler-Ross gives an example of a patient at the bargaining stage who asked for enough time to attend her eldest son's wedding. She left the hospital the day of the wedding, returned the next day, and began bargaining for enough time to attend her second son's wedding.

An anticipated or actual physical loss usually brings on the fourth postulated stage—*depression*. Depression may be the result of increased symptoms or the realization that one is becoming weaker and thinner. Surgical procedures such as the removal of a breast or part of the face often result in deep depression. According to Kübler-Ross, a patient should be encouraged to work through this anguish and, in so doing, reach the final stage in the dying process—*acceptance*. "If a patient has had enough time. . .and has been given some help in working through the previously described stages, he will reach a state during which he is neither depressed nor angry about his 'fate'."

Kübler-Ross completed her analysis with the observation that a little hope runs through all five stages and that patients are aware of the seriousness of their illness whether or not they are so informed. All patients, according to Kübler-Ross, have the opportunity to work through the stages and achieve a good death. Although some patients reach the acceptance stage without the aid of others, most need assistance. The Kübler-Ross message then is that medical personnel and family members should be sensitive to whatever stage a dying patient is in and, if necessary, work with the patient to reach the acceptance stage.

Unfortunately, the usefulness of Kübler-Ross's work is limited by its ambiguity, which is largely a product of the highly subjective manner in which her observations were obtained and interpreted. Kübler-Ross failed to explicitly specify assessment procedures for identifying the stages of dying. Judging from the interview protocols Kübler-Ross presented in support of her stage model, it appears that she depended more on intuition to define a particular stage than on any systematic pattern of responses from the patient. Because misperceiving a stage could result in negative consequences for the patient (e.g., earlier death), it is crucial that the stages be clearly and easily identified. It is also important to know whether dying patients necessarily go through each stage in the particular sequence or whether they jump from one stage to another, skipping one or more in between. Clearly, the stages have little predictive value and perhaps little practical value if one cannot easily specify the stage an individual is in and the stage that is to follow.

While Kübler-Ross based her conclusions on information obtained through highly subjective personal interaction with over 200 dying patients, other researchers (Hinton, 1963; Achte and Vauhkonen, 1971; Lieberman, 1965; Weisman and Kastenbaum, 1968; Kastenbaum and Weisman, 1972) have attempted to plot the emotional trajectory of the dying patient with more objective methods. Hinton (1963), for example, assessed mood, physical distress, level of consciousness, and awareness of dying in approximately 70 dying patients who were interviewed at weekly intervals. Data collected during the last eight weeks each patient lived were analyzed.

A large portion of the sample (nearly 90 percent) experienced physical distress, which required the administration of "a popular and effective mixture of morphine and cocaine" (Hinton, 1963). Although Hinton acknowledged that the drug may have produced side-effects, such as altered mood and decreased level of consciousness, he made no attempt to document the extent of this influence. Among all patients, impairment of consciousness increased steadily from 20 percent at the eighth week to 55 percent shortly before death. Among those patients who remained conscious, depression was found in half the patients throughout the eight weeks, and it increased during the last two weeks of life. Anxiety was less prevalent, but showed a similar increase in the last two weeks of life.

Expectations of death were generally low among conscious patients. Only 20 percent of these patients were certain that they were going to die a week before death while another 20 percent thought that death was probable within this time period. The remaining patients had not mentioned death at all or had spoken only of the possibility of dying.

Since Hinton and Kübler-Ross both used nondirected interviews to collect their data, their results should be comparable. Both investigators observed increased depression shortly before death, but only Hinton acknowledged the possibility that drugs may have influenced this finding. Undoubtedly Kübler-Ross's patients were conscious when interviewed, but some of them may have been taking drugs which altered their mood. The depression she associated with the increased severity of physical symptoms, for instance, may simply have been the result of increased doses of drugs given to alleviate the new or more severe symptoms.

Hinton assessed general anxiety as a separate dimension in his patients; Kübler-Ross viewed it as something that is present in many patients throughout several of the early stages but not in the final acceptance stage. Since Hinton found increased anxiety shortly before death, the data from the two studies do not agree here. Another disparity is the patient's awareness of his or her condition. Kübler-Ross reported that all of her patients knew they were terminal, while Hinton claimed that only 40 percent of his patients felt that their death was probable. Perhaps the other 60 percent of Hinton's patients also knew of their impending death but were merely denying it. If this is true, then another disparity comes to light: patients who, according to Kübler-Ross, should be at or near the acceptance stage are still denying, according to Hinton.

Regardless of interpretation, it is difficult to reconcile the two sets of observations. One might argue that such disparities are to be expected given different populations of patients, but such an argument negates the general usefulness of this line of research.

Achte and Vauhkonen (1971) compared a group of terminal cancer patients with a group of nonterminal controls who also had cancer. The higher frequency of depression in the terminal group was the biggest difference between the two groups, although anxiety and tension were also more frequent among terminal patients. These findings are generally consistent with those reported by Hinton and Kübler-Ross. Aggressiveness was frequently observed in the subgroup whose illness terminated quickly. These aggressive patients most closely resembled Kübler-Ross's patients in the denial and anger stages. Apparently, however, their deaths occurred before they had passed through the remaining Kübler-Ross stages.

Consistent with Hinton's findings, 50 percent of those patients who died were unaware of the nature of their illness. Again, lack of awareness can be interpreted as repression or denial.

Lieberman (1965) studied 25 men and women volunteers from a home for the aged. Subjects were given a series of tests and questionnaires at three-to-four-week intervals over a two-and-one-half-year period. Since eight of his subjects died after the study was begun, he was able to go back and determine whether or not the responses of subjects who died (Death Imminent Group—DIG) differed from those who did not die (Death Delayed Group—DDG).

The assessment devices included the Bender-Gestalt Test, the Draw-a-Person Test, a time reproduction task, and a projective test in which the subject was asked to respond to 12 line drawings. With these tools Lieberman hoped to measure ego and cognitive functioning and affective states over time. Only his significant findings will be discussed here.

At the time of first measurement, the two groups were found to differ significantly on only the area score of the Bender-Gestalt Test; the DIG had an initially smaller score than the DDG. Presumably this is an indication that the DIG had less "available energy that is free for dealing with stimuli from the outer world." That is, they were unable to cope adequately with environmental demands. The results could not be accounted for by differences in physical illness.

The most significant finding of this study was the marked change in the DIG's performance relative to their initial scores. According to Lieberman, these subjects showed a "decreased level of organization as measured by the adequacy of the Bender-Gestalt reproductions, a decreased energy as indicated by measurement of the size of the Bender-Gestalt figures, and a lessened ability to integrate stimuli as shown by a decrease in the complexity of the figure drawings." Only affective states, as measured by the projective technique, were not systematically related to approaching death. Lieberman attributed the decreased ability of individuals in the DIG to organize and integrate stimuli to a "general system decline," which is reflected in a variety of physiological and psychological measures. Their ability to receive external stimuli did not decrease, but their ability to interpret and deal with these stimuli was impaired, leaving them with the frightening impression that they were at the mercy of a chaotic world.

Lieberman used this same line of reasoning to explain the tendency for individuals approaching death to draw away from others and to isolate themselves. In his view, they do not withdraw because of "narcissistic preoccupation with themselves, but because they are preoccupied in an attempt to hold themselves together—to reduce the experience of chaos."

It is likely that the behavior Lieberman describes as *cognitive withdrawal* is interpreted as depression by other investigators. If this is the case, then the four studies reviewed here agree on one thing—that is, all terminal patients exhibit withdrawal or depression shortly before dying. Three related explanations for this behavior have been suggested. Kübler-Ross claimed that patients become depressed when they experience an increase in the severity of symptoms or the loss of some body part. Lieberman felt that depression may have its source in the physical decline that results in decreased ability to make sense of and deal with environmental stimuli, while Hinton believed that depression was drug-related. Probably all three factors operate.

With the exception of the data on withdrawal, Lieberman's results differ from all the other data presented in that he found no affective differences between the death-imminent group and the death-delayed group; nor did he find any temporal changes in affective states of patients in the DIG.

Two methodological features of Lieberman's study may have contributed to his rather unique findings. First, Lieberman used a projective test rather than a direct interview to assess the affective state. The interviewer was more likely to become intimate with the patient and learn more about his or her feelings in the direct interviews. Given the formality of Lieberman's tests and the fact that his interviewers were replaced halfway through the study, it is unlikely that the patient grew close to his or her interviewer.

Secondly, Lieberman administered his tests at three-to-four-week intervals over a two-and-one-half-year period, while the intervals were much shorter in Hinton's and Kübler-Ross's studies. Hinton collected data at weekly intervals, and Kübler-Ross presumably visited her patients everyday. It is possible that affective changes occurred in the Lieberman study, but remained undetected.

A very different approach to the study of the terminal phase of life has been taken by Weisman and Kastenbaum (1968). Using a procedure called the *psychological autopsy*, these authors attempted to reconstruct the final phases in the life of a patient. Their procedure involved interdisciplinary conferences in which information about a recently deceased patient was presented and discussed with the aim of studying the psychosocial context in which the death occurred.

After reviewing 80 cases over a five year period, Weisman and Kastenbaum (1968) concluded that patients entering the terminal period could be separated into two groups on the basis of their responses to impending death. One group seemed to be aware of and to accept impending death. Most of these patients withdrew from daily activities and remained inactive until the end. The other group was also aware of imminent death but vigorously engaged in daily life activities and even initiated new activities and interpersonal relationships. Death for these individuals came as an interruption in daily living. Fear of dying was observed rarely and then only in patients who were grossly impaired.

Kastenbaum and Weisman (1972) reported a similar pattern of responses in another sample of 35 cases. They found that the group that withdrew contained older individuals (89 vs. 81.5 years) and had a shorter hospital stay (20 vs. 37.5 months) before death than the group that remained active. Since data on cognitive functioning are not reported perhaps the two patterns of behavior are partly the result of different levels of cognitive ability. Like Lieberman's DIG patients, the older group may have withdrawn because they were less capable of coping with their environment while the younger group still had the capacity and motivation to engage in everyday activities.

Although these data were collected and interpreted post hoc and must therefore be viewed with caution, the findings again cast doubt on the validity of a stage theory. Patients were not observed to go through stages but rather to adopt a pattern of behavior that persisted until death.

MEETING THE NEEDS OF THE DYING

For the most part, we have focused in this chapter on affective states associated with the terminal phase of life and little has been said about the specific needs of the dying patient. Although a large variety of needs are talked about in the literature, there is a consensus among most writers on the subject that the following are the three major needs of terminal patients:

1   the need to control pain;

2   the need to retain dignity or feelings of self worth; and

3   the need for love and affection.

Need to control pain

Probably the most important need of the dying patient is the need to control the pain associated with terminal disease. Drug therapy and surgical procedures are the primary available antidotes for pain, but the patient must pay a price for both—that is, either decreased mobility with surgical procedures or altered states of consciousness with drugs. Drugs are more commonly used.

Since medical practitioners and patients do not have to worry about the social consequences of addiction, drugs such as morphine and diamorphine are commonly used to control pain. In administering these drugs, however, the medical practitioner must confront the issue of who is to determine the dosage of a drug the patient is to receive. Ultimately, it is the physician who makes the decision, but it can be argued that the patient's opinion should be considered as well, since she or he is intimately aware of her or his own pain tolerance, as well as the fluctuations of internal states. If possible, the medical staff and the patient should be able to anticipate and prevent pain rather than alleviate it (Neale, 1971). The medical staff at St. Christopher's Hospice in London use this strategy successfully.

When heroin is administered, this means the use of low and frequent dosages. One notable side effect of heroin is general euphoria and some practitioners have argued that since the patient in pain is far below the normal level of functioning, the drug simply brings her or him back up to normal functioning (Neale, 1971).

Alcohol (e.g., beer, wine, hard liquor) is another option available for the control of pain. As is the case with heroin, the side effects of alcohol appear to contribute to normal patient functioning. Marijuana is also occasionally prescribed as an antidote for pain and nausea (Kavanaugh, 1974).

The use of LSD for pain relief in terminal patients started in the early 1960s, when Eric Kast, an anesthesiologist at Cook County Hospital in Chicago, administered it to 128 terminal cancer patients who were in great pain. LSD proved to be as effective in alleviating pain as the usual opiates, and its effect lasted longer. Indeed, the pain relief continued even after the LSD trip terminated. Even after the pain returned, some patients retained their equanimity; they no longer considered their pain *important*.

Eric Kast's work with LSD and cancer patients was further pursued by Sidney Cohen, Walter Pahnke, and Albert Kurl and at the Maryland Psychiatric Research Center in Cantonsville, near Baltimore (Avorn, 1973). The research was launched under dramatic circumstances when a research assistant who developed inoperable cancer requested LSD therapy. The patient vividly described the procedure and the experience of her LSD trip (Brecher, 1972).

In the treatment room was a beautiful happiness rosebud, deep red and dewy, but disappointingly not as fragrant as other varieties. A bowl of fruit, moist, succulent, also reposed on the table. I was immediately given the first dose and sat looking at pictures from my family album. Gradually my movements became fuzzy and I felt awkward. I was made to recline with earphones and eyeshades. At some point, the second LSD dose was given me. . .it seems I fused with the music and was transported on it. So completely was I one with the sound that when the particular melody or record stopped, however momentarily, I was alive to the pause, eagerly awaiting the next lap in the journey. A delightful game was being played. I felt at these times I was being teased, but so nicely, so gently. I wanted to laugh in sheer appreciation. . . .Life reduced itself over and over again to the least common denominator. I cannot remember the logic of the experience, but I became poignantly aware that the core of life is love. At this point I felt I was reaching out to the world—to all people—but especially to those closest to me. I wept for the wasted years, the search for identity in false places, the neglected opportunities, the emotional energy lost in basically meaningless pursuits. . .

Later (after the LSD therapy), all noticed a change in me. I was radiant, they said. I seemed at peace. What has changed for me? I am living now, and being. I can take it as it comes. Some of my physical symptoms are gone. The excessive fatigue, some of the pains. I still get irritated occasionally and yell. I am still me, but more at peace. My family senses this and we are closer. All who know me well say that this has been a good experience.

Psychological tests given this patient before and after LSD therapy indicated a significant reduction in depression and other pathological signs. The patient returned to work and lived in relatively good spirits for five weeks after which she was hospitalized and quickly died.

It is generally believed that the perception of pain has two components—the physical sensation itself, which we can never completely know, and the psychological interpretation of that sensation. LSD appears to affect the latter while the opiates affect the physical sensation itself.

From the researcher's point of view, it is unfortunate that the effects of LSD therapy have not been studied using placebos and double-blind procedures. It is difficult to determine from the available reports whether the results can be attributed to the drug or to the therapeutic attention accompanying the procedure. But from an ethical perspective, such research may be unjustified

Need for dignity

Once pain is controlled, attention can be focused on enhancing the patient's feeling of dignity or self-worth. Sister Mary Louise Nash (1975) describes dignity as a sense of self-worth, a sense of stature, goodness, self-respect, and being liked for one's self. Dignity comes from the patient's participation in decisions affecting his or her outcomes. Control over the terminal phase of one's life is at least as important as control over the rest of one's life.

A growing literature in experimental social psychology demonstrates the importance of control as a mediator of perception of competence, self-worth, and associated affective states such as depression.

Seligman (1975) convincingly argues that feelings of hopelessness and helplessness result when individuals feel themselves unable to control their outcomes. Experiments with both animals and humans have demonstrated that prolonged experiences of noncontingency (i.e., lack of effectiveness in controlling one's outcomes) results in cognitive, emotional, and motivational deficits. Organisms perform poorly, are more likely to give up in subsequent situations, and exhibit withdrawal and depression.

In my own work with the aged (Schulz, 1976a), I have found that loss of control—from decreased mobility and financial status, loss of the work and child rearing roles, loss of freedom after institutionalization—was psychologically as well as physically devastating. In a field experiment, some institutionalized aged individuals were given the opportunity to increase their control over an aspect of their environment; this significantly improved their psychological and physical status when compared to other aged individuals who were randomly assigned to conditions and did not have the opportunity to exert control. The terminal patient's plight is especially difficult in that physical limitations have drastically reduced his or her effectiveness in manipulating his or her environment. Perhaps even more important, the terminal patient must live with the realization that soon his or her impact will be reduced to zero.

How can we give the terminal patient the feeling that she or he is still an effective force in her or his environment? Probably the easiest way to accomplish this is to make the terminal patient a participant in his or her treatment program rather than the object of a program contrived by the medical staff. The patient's participation, however, makes sense only if she or he is knowledgeable about her or his condition and the alternatives available. This, in turn, raises an important issue that was discussed earlier in this chapter. Should the terminal patient be informed of her or his condition?

Recall that the three prevalent stands on the issue are the following:

1 a small group of physicians who advocate a "play-it-by-ear" policy;

2   the majority of practicing physicians who engage in a policy of benign neglect; and

3   the patients themselves, who for the most part desire such information and suffer no long term adverse effects as a result of being told of their condition.

We concluded earlier that most patients should be informed of their condition, although this should be carried out with sensitivity and tact. Given the necessity of informing the patient in order to make him or her an active participant in his or her treatment, I now argue that *all* patients should be informed of their condition. Preserving the patient's dignity by recognizing him or her as a legitimate participant in decisions concerning his or her treatment, I believe, outweighs the usual short-term trauma the patient experiences when being informed about his or her condition. In addition to directly involving the patient in his or her treatment, the patient may also benefit from having control over the intensity and quality of his or her social contact with other individuals. The patient should be encouraged to stipulate what kinds of interaction she or he wants, with whom, and when.

To conclude, just as dignity and feelings of self-worth are enhanced for nonterminal patients by allowing them to perceive themselves as effective agents in their environment, dignity for terminal patients is preserved by allowing them some control in their environment. The tricky part of this is that the terminal patient's environment has traditionally been controlling rather than controlled, and therefore significant changes in the attitudes of medical practitioners are necessary for positive change.

Need for love and affection

It is probably true that you have to love yourself before you can feel that others love you. Loving yourself usually requires self-respect, feelings of goodness, and self-worth. Thus, it appears that the benefits of love are maximized after the individual's need for dignity has been fulfilled.

For the terminal patient, love and affection are usually expressed by physical contact—touching, stroking, holding, feeling another's breath. *Touching* is an inevitable part of medical and nursing care, but it is the extra touch that communicates love. Touching is an important feature of the patient-staff relationships at St. Christopher's Hospice.

The staff are encouraged to sit with the patient on her or his bed and engage in physical contact. Love also involves the ability to listen, perceive, and follow the patient's own approach to her or his dilemma with assurances that she or he will not be abandoned.

The hospice as an alternative

The *hospice approach* to the treatment of terminal patients has recently been instituted in the United States (Holden, 1976). At present, the National Cancer Institute is supporting a hospice located in New Haven, Connecticut, that is modeled after St. Christopher's Hospice in London. The Connecticut hospice began as a home-care program and eventually evolved into a 44-bed resident facility, tailored to replicate the essential aspects of the program at St. Christopher's. What are the critical aspects of such a program? A partial answer to this question has already been presented. We have discussed how the staff at St. Christopher's help patients control their pain and provide love.

More specifically, an anti-pain cocktail, called *Brompton's mixture*, is used. It is made up of diamorphine (heroin), cocaine, gin, sugar syrup, and chlorpromazine syrup. (In the United States, morphine is substituted for heroin.) Initial doses of heroin range from 5 to 10 milligrams and may eventually go as high as 30 milligrams at a time. According to Cicely Saunders, director of St. Christopher's, dosages of heroin often decrease over time, once a patient's fears and anxieties about pain are relieved. There is no such thing as giving "too much" of an analgesic, and patients rarely take quantities that turn them into insensate zombies.

Complementing the pain-control program is a loving and caring atmosphere, created by the constant attention rendered by staff and volunteers, who along with friends and relatives spend much time just listening to patients and holding their hands, as well as engaging in other types of physical contact. Visiting hours are not as restricted as they are in hospitals so that family and friends can spend as much time with the patient as they desire.

A final characteristic of the hospice approach is that in the process of treating the patient, the family is simultaneously treated. By including family members in the treatment program, relatives have the opportunity not only to work through their relationship with the patient, but also to perform practical services for the dying such as preparing special meals. This type of participation effectively minimizes feelings of guilt during bereavement. Moreover, the staff's involvement with the relatives and friends does not end with the patient's death. Friends and relatives of the deceased are encouraged to consult with the staff should they run into difficulties during bereavement.

Ultimately, the success of the hospice movement in the United States will depend on two factors: (1) the cost of treatment and (2) its success in meeting its stated goals. The available data suggest that care received in a hospice will be less expensive than general hospital care for the dying. For example, at St. Christopher's Hospice in England, the cost per patient is 80 percent of that of a general hospital.

According to Frank Kryza, director of information at Hospice Inc. in New Haven, Connecticut, similar and perhaps even greater savings should be realized in the United States. He claims savings of $1800 per patient in the home-care program because patients are able to spend an average of two weeks less in the hospital as part of their home-care program. This represents a very substantial cost reduction and at the same time increases the patient's probability of dying at home in familiar surroundings.

Is the hospice program likely to work in the United States? Those who are familiar with and speak and write about the hospice movement do so with a zealotry that "turns off" rather than "turns on" potential converts. Their enthusiasm is understandable, but it should perhaps be tinged with a little cautiousness in selling the hospice idea. Thus those who are fighting for the program may be their own worst enemies.

Stronger reservations about the hospice program have been voiced by some individuals. Mel Krant, director of cancer programs at the University of Massachusetts School of Medicine in Worcester, feels that hospices will add to "excessive fragmentation, overspecialization, and discontinuity in American medicine" (Holden, 1976). What is needed is greater integration of medical services. An alternative approach to the hospice idea might be to use existing institutions (e.g., hospitals) and to increase efforts at staff education on fulfilling the needs of the dying.

There is in addition the danger of hospices becoming glorified nursing homes. Without the spirit of volunteerism and utterly devoted leaders, such as Cicely Saunders, a hospice could easily function like an expensive nursing home. Finally, there is the potential of the limited-resource problem. If the hospices do become successful and if the demand for their services becomes greater than the available resources, how will bed space be allocated? Who will decide who does or doesn't qualify for hospice care?

These are undoubtedly only some of the problems and issues confronting the hospice movement in the United States. One fact is incontrovertible:—that is, *the existing facilities and techniques for the treatment of the dying in the United States are in need of improvement.*

Research and other alternatives to care

Two unique treatment programs have been mentioned in this discussion; St. Christopher's Hospice in London and the LSD therapy program in Cantonsville, Maryland. In addition to these, numerous more traditional programs using art therapy, music therapy, and various forms of group therapy can be found around the country. In fact, any of the tools of the clinical psychologist are appropriate for the treatment of the dying patient.

Given that all these techniques are available, how might we best choose among them? Research is necessary to answer this. Being trained as an experimental social psychologist, the thought that immediately comes to mind when I think about research is, "What are the independent and dependent variables in this situation?" The former question is relatively easy to answer. We can assess a multitude of individual differences and make a detailed assessment of the patient's past history. We can examine her or his social network and assess the quantity and quality of significant persons in her or his life. The patient's socioeconomic status, past experience with stressful events, ability to cope with stressful events, the type of institution, and characteristics of the medical staff can all serve as independent variables.

The difficult part of this assignment is the selection of the dependent measures. Should we simply obtain self-reports from the patient about how he or she feels psychologically and physically at a given time? Years of social psychological research have taught us that self-report measures are often poor indicators of what's really going on. Perhaps some unobtrusive measures of well-being or satisfaction would serve as more valid indicators of the patient's condition. Verbal utterances as well as nonverbal acts might be classified as expressing either negative or positive states and tallied to quantitatively assess the patient's affective state. Unobtrusive measures such as these can also be used to check the validity of self-report measures.

After clearly specifying the independent and dependent variables, the researcher must decide on the research technique. Research on the psychological aspects of the terminal phase of life is still in its infancy and, at the beginning stages of knowledge-gathering, non- and quasi-experimental designs are highly desirable. Such designs are usually less costly and under some circumstances are the only types of designs that can be carried out. Most of the existing research on the terminal phase of life is descriptive or correlational and leaves questions of causality unanswered.

Given what we already know about terminal patients, I believe that future research efforts should concentrate on correlational and—if ethically and logistically possible—on experimental techniques. For example, I think there is little more to be learned about pain control by administering a drug to a population of patients and compiling detailed descriptions on the effect of the drug in relieving pain. Double-blind procedures are necessary to objectively assess the effect of a drug given to relieve pain. Similarly, the issue of whether or not to inform a patient of his or her terminality (if indeed that is still an issue) will be difficult to resolve until an experimental procedure is used, whereby subjects are randomly assigned to conditions in which some receive the information and others do not. The importance of environmental control as an enhancer of dignity could also be tested by an experimental procedure.

This is the kind of research that *could* be carried out, but I'm not sure it *should* be carried out. Experimental research raises important ethical issues. For example, does the experimenter have the right to deprive some patients of a treatment that she or he thinks *may* be beneficial? Clearly, in an experimental study, only manipulations that are expected to have positive effects are permissible and under no circumstances should a patient be deprived of an established service for the benefit of research. However, it is justifiable in my mind to carry out experimental research if the control group for the study receives "treatment as usual" and if the experimental group or groups are exposed to a manipulation that is expected to have beneficial effects.

Conclusion

Alban Wheeler (1973) has argued that the dying person is a deviant in the medical subculture. Much of the research reviewed above supports this view. The dying person elicits aversive attitudes from the people around him or her, and these attitudes often result in avoidance behaviors on the part of physicians and nurses. Future research should be aimed at documenting medical staff interactions with dying patients as well as investigating ways in which attitudes of practitioners might be changed, should change be necessary. One possible approach to changing the attitudes of practitioners might be to convince medical and nursing schools to focus on the social-psychological aspects of death and dying as part of their curriculum.

Although we know something about the emotional trajectory of the dying patient, the disparity in current findings indicates that more information is needed. At present, we know that the dying patient's physical and cognitive functions deteriorate and he or she characteristically becomes depressed and perhaps anxious about dying. Much more research is needed for a satisfactory understanding of the emotional aspects of this last phase of life.

EUTHANASIA

The problem of prolonging the life of the terminal patient or alleviating her or his discomfort culminates in the euthanasia question. Medical technology has advanced to the point where machines can maintain all vital systems except the brain. The public and the medical profession are beginning to realize that the technology designed to save the lives of critically ill persons may not be appropriate for terminally ill patients. This raises profound moral, legal, and ethical issues, which will be examined in detail in this section.

The word *euthanasia* is derived from Latin, *eu*, meaning good, and *thanasia* meaning death. Euthanasia is defined as the act or practice of killing for reasons of mercy—popularly called *mercy killing*. Two types of euthanasia are recognized in medical and legal circles—passive and active.

Passive euthanasia refers to situations in which an individual dies because she or he is allowed to die or because available preventive measures are not used to keep her or him alive. That is, a treatment may be withheld or withdrawn so that the patient is likely to die earlier than she or he would have if she or he had received treatment. Consider, for example, a terminal cancer patient who is suffering from intense pain and who contracts pneumonia. Left untreated, the pneumonia will more than likely result in the patient's death. The physician confronted with such a situation has the choice of either treating the pain, or the pneumonia, or both. Treating both simultaneously is sometimes difficult or impossible since a treatment program for one condition may be harmful for the other. In this example, the physician who treats the pain by administering morphine and withholding penicillin or antibiotics which would cure the pneumonia is practicing passive euthanasia. The moral, ethical, and legal issues raised by such behavior will be discussed later.

Active euthanasia is most commonly practiced by local animal protection societies. Cats and dogs are routinely killed when homes cannot be found for them. Presumably, these animals are better off dead than eking out a miserable existence in the streets; by killing them, we save them from an arduous life and at the same time eliminate a nuisance from our own. Similarly, veterinarians are often asked to end the life of an ailing pet to save it from a protracted period of pain and suffering. The essence of active euthanasia is that something is deliberately done to shorten an organism's life; this includes such acts as the injection of air bubbles or the administration of a fast-acting poison. However, the distinction between active and passive euthanasia is not always clear and not everyone believes that they are medically or morally different.

Current usage and opinions on euthanasia

Public opinion on euthanasia has changed considerably in the last two decades. In 1950, 36 percent of the population answered "yes" when asked as part of a Gallup poll, "When a person has a disease that cannot be cured, do you think doctors should be allowed by law to end the patient's life by some painless means if the patient and his family request it?" In 1973, the percent of the population responding "yes" had increased to 53, with Catholics agreeing slightly less (48 percent) than the population as a whole.

A similar poll, conducted in 1969 on members of the American Physicians Association, revealed that 87 percent of physicians replying approved of passive euthanasia and 80 percent admitted practicing it. (It should be noted that in practice only a small minority of patients have everything possible done for their survival until the moment of death. Thus it might be argued that passive euthanasia is more often the rule than the exception.) In 1973, at the convention of the American

Medical Association, physicians backed a *death with dignity proposition* and supported the use of *living wills*, which allow people to choose their own fate in situations where death may be imminent (*Science News*, 1973).

A recent article presented the views of two famous physicians on who should decide when to let terminal patients die. The question addressed by these physicians is not *if* a decision should be made but *who* should decide. Dr. Christiaan Barnard feels that the doctor, not the patient or his or her family, is the only one in the position to decide the fate of a terminal patient. The patient, he argues, can't discuss his or her own death, and the family should not be burdened with such decisions. The implication is that ending a person's life is a medical, technical decision and not a personal one. The opposite point of view is argued by Dr. Edmund Pellegrino; he states that the patient and/or his or her family should always be consulted so that the doctor can't subject others to his or her values about life. *This implies that death is a personal matter.* As discussed earlier, my views are more consistent with Pellegrino's, but for somewhat different reasons.

The legal view of euthanasia is generally murky. The law does not recognize the "mercy" aspect of mercy killing. Most euthanasia cases are tried as murder cases. Maguire (1974b) argues that euthanasia cannot be murder or manslaughter of any degree. Murder is characterized by *express malice* in the first degree and *implied malice* in the second degree. Manslaughter is defined as a sudden or unintentional killing without malice. Although euthanasia may be carried out with intent, it is not carried out with malice, implied or direct, toward the patient. Other countries—West Germany, Uruguay, and Switzerland—have legal provisions for intentional killing without malice; the laws in this country have no such provisions.

Although the laws in the United States are somewhat insensitive to the motives of the individual in euthanasia cases, and prosecutors typically stress that honorable motives cannot be considered in a murder case, juries have been very sensitive to such motives and are often reluctant to convict. For example, in two cases where doctors were tried for the murder of dying patients, neither was convicted. Dr. Vincent A. Montemarano was accused of injecting a dying patient with a lethal dose of medication. In 1950, Dr. Sanders, a country doctor from New Hampshire, was accused of injecting air into a terminally ill patient (Maguire, 1974a). Both doctors were acquitted.

More common are trials of family members accused of killing a suffering relative. In many cases, the suffering person asked or begged to be killed. There is little standard procedure in such cases, and verdicts have ranged from first-degree murder to acquittal or acquittal by temporary insanity. In most cases, however, public opinion dominates, and the accused are acquitted.

The euthanasia issue was again raised by the recent Karen Ann Quinlan case.

Karen had been in a deep, irreversible coma for seven months when her parents requested that the respirator that was keeping her alive be shut off. The attending doctors would not shut off the respirator because they feared legal problems. The New Jersey court denied the Quinlan's request, stating that Karen was legally and medically alive, saying, "Humanitarian motives cannot justify the taking of a human life."

In April 1976, after Karen had been in a coma for one year, the Superior Court unanimously struck down the earlier decision and set a new precedent concerning terminal illness. "The state's interest (in preserving life) weakens and the individual's right to privacy grows as the degree of bodily invasion increases and the prognosis dims. Ultimately there comes a point at which the individual's rights overcome the state's interest." The court instructed that the respirator could be turned off if "there is no reasonable possibility" that she will return to a "cognitive, sapient state" (Seligmann, 1976). The court further stated that these standards apply to all whose condition is progressive and incurable.

This decision made it possible to shut off the respirator, but the story doesn't end there. Karen Ann Quinlan is still alive at this writing, still in a coma, and breathing unaided.

Religious views on euthanasia vary widely across different religions and within specific religious sects. For example, a gamut of opinions can be found among Protestants, ranging from active euthanasia to "save every last bit of life at all costs." There is no one standard for all factions. The emphasis is placed on personal choice and discretion; there are no hard and fast rules. *Love thy neighbor* is as important as *Thou shalt not kill* (Shideler, 1966).

The Catholic dictum on euthanasia was voiced in 1957 by Pope Pius XII, who recognized the potential moral problems raised by the availability of life-sustaining technology and stated that Catholics are not morally obligated to use *extraordinary measures* to keep hopelessly ill persons alive. He did not, however, offer a clear definition of extraordinary measures (Maguire, 1974a).

The Jewish position on euthanasia is relatively straightforward (Sherwin, 1975). It is derived from ancient Jewish law and stresses that life is intrinsically sacred and should be preserved, even at great cost. The dying person is considered living in all respects and no effort should be made to hasten his death. Suicide or any self-injury is strictly prohibited under all circumstances. Passive euthanasia is permitted in the sense that it is permissible to remove artificial means of keeping a dying person alive. Active euthanasia is strictly prohibited.

Conclusions and alternatives

There are many reasons why a terminal patient (and/or his or her family) may desire death:

1　Severe and/or unrelieved pain
2　Mental distress, depression, and isolation
3　The belief that life is no longer meaningful
4　Desire for a dignified death
5　Desire to control when and how one dies
6　A desire to avoid becoming an emotional or financial burden on the family
7　Finances

Most of these are valid reasons because they are directed at fulfilling the special needs of the dying patient. Only the last two reasons—finances and the desire not to be a burden—are potential exceptions to this. It is conceivable that a terminal patient may find himself or herself in a situation where he or she receives very subtle or even direct cues from friends or relatives communicating their wish that the patient die. If these wishes conflict with the patient's, he or she may be placed in the position of opting prematurely for his or her own death. While such conflicts might be rare, even if the practice of euthanasia became commonplace, it is essential to recognize this possibility.

It is likely that personal control over one's death will increase in the near future. The concept of a legally binding "Living Will" that would extend the individual's control over her or his body and life has been recently introduced. The purpose of such a will is to stipulate what should be done for the individual should she or he become unconscious or mentally incompetent to decide her or his own fate. An individual might, for example, stipulate that if she or he goes into an apparent irreversible coma, no heroic efforts be used to sustain life. With such a will the physician would be free to carry out the individual's wishes without fear of legal or medical censure.

The euthanasia issue is an important one and will undoubtedly continue to grow in importance as medical technology improves and attitudes toward life and death change. We have limited the discussion here to euthanasia as it relates to the dying patient. Other questions can be raised. For example, how far should euthanasia be extended? To deformed infants, the senile, the mentally ill? These questions are beyond the scope of this book but are in need of close scrutiny.

DEFINING DEATH

Death is a process, not a moment. Cells within the body are dying all the time. Even after an individual has been determined legally dead, the body remains almost entirely alive. As Kastenbaum and Aisenberg (1972) put it, "Just as there may be local death in a living body, so there may be local life in a dead body."

Determining whether someone is alive or dead has been a tricky business since earliest times. The major indicators are, as they have always been, spontaneous respiration and heartbeat. However, with the recent introduction of life-sustaining technical devices, the validity of these indicators has been questioned. On the one hand, technology has provided numerous ways of sensing the faintest pulse or breath, and so has made detecting the absence of these signs easier and more reliable. On the other hand, technology has provided respirators, heart-lung machines, etc., that can directly support all vital systems except the brain. What does it mean, then, to be *physically dead*?

Three types of death have been identified.

1   *Clinical death* is said to occur when spontaneous respiration and heartbeat cease. Resuscitation may be attempted and in some cases will revive the individual. An example of the latter case is an individual who suffers a major heart attack and is promptly given emergency treatment to resuscitate her or him.

2   *Brain death* is a second type of death. If deprived of oxygen (anoxia), brain cells begin to die within four to six minutes if the person is not resuscitated immediately. The most highly evolved part of the brain, the cortex, dies first. This part of the brain is involved in controlling voluntary action, thought, and memory. The midbrain dies next, followed by the death of the oldest part of the brain, the brainstem. If the cortex and midbrain are destroyed, the person lapses into an irreversible coma and only the vegetative functions remain. Thus an individual could be in a deep coma and still be able to breathe unaided, and, with the aid of intravenous feeding, he or she could remain alive almost indefinitely.

3   *Biological or cellular death*, the physical death of the various organ systems, occurs last. Different organs die at different rates and an organ is defined as dead when it has degenerated to a point where any type of intervention would not bring it back to a functional state again.

Researchers and doctors have recently turned to the brain in their search for new death criteria since the brain is the only system that cannot be directly supported by machines. The concept of brain death as one of the major criteria for death has become popular in recent years. In 1968, the Harvard Ad Hoc Committee to Examine the Definition of Brain Death proposed the following operational criteria: unreceptivity and unresponsivity, no movements or breathing, no reflexes, and a flat electroencephalogram (EEG) reading that remains flat for 24 hours (Veatch, 1976). The committee members referred to this state as an *irreversible coma*. It should be noted that the combination of criteria and not just a flat EEG are necessary to classify an individual as being in an irreversible coma. A flat EEG record can also result from drastically lowering the body temperature, certain injuries, and ingesting alcohol with drugs such as heroin, barbituates, or tranquilizers.

In some cases, individuals can be resuscitated. The Harvard committee examined 503 persons who appeared to be in irreversible comas. Aside from 44, who had flat EEG readings because of these special conditions, none of the others (459) ever recovered. The Harvard Ad Hoc Committee. The Kansas and Maryland state legislatures have also adopted a similar standard.

The Karen Ann Quinlan case highlights the distinction between reversible and irreversible comas. Her coma was probably drug induced. She was thought to be in an irreversible coma until the respirators keeping her alive were removed. Since she began breathing under her own powers, there is some possibility that her coma is reversible, although medical opinion is divided about the possibility of her regaining any other functions.

Some researchers and practitioners believe that the Harvard criteria are already outmoded, and prefer the concept of *cerebral death*. Death, by this definition, occurs when the higher brain center, the cortex, is irreversibly destroyed; the patient is completely and forever unconscious but may still be able to breathe unaided with the vegetative functions intact. Applying these standards, Karen Ann Quinlan would be considered dead. This is at present, a controversial position because if a person can breathe unaided, he or she is still "alive" by all traditional standards. People who support the idea of cerebral death feel that the cortex—which holds the capacity for thought, voluntary action, and memory—*is the individual* and, when consciousness is gone, the individual is no longer a person.

The technological advances that have made organ transplants possible have added another dimension to the semantics of death. Since hearts, lungs, and kidneys must be taken from the donor's body as soon as possible after the blood flow has been halted, a precise definition of death is legally necessary. With a respirator oxygenating the blood and a pump pulsing it through the donor's body, determining the moment of death becomes increasingly difficult. While a transplant cannot be carried out until the donor has been declared dead, ambiguity in defining the moment of death has resulted in some interesting court cases. One such case (Hendin, 1973) occurred in 1968, in Houston, Texas.

Denton Cooley, a surgeon, performed a heart transplant at Houston's St. Luke's Hospital. Clarence Nicks, the heart donor, had been badly beaten in a barroom brawl. By the time he was delivered to the hospital his brain registered no electrical activity and he had no reflexes. His condition did not change for several hours. The machine providing oxygen to his blood was turned off, and his heart was transplanted to John Stuchwish, who lived for several days after the transplant.

Since the legally valid autopsy necessary in homicide cases was not carried out, there was some concern among physicians and lawyers about whether the trial of Nicks's assailant might be affected by the removal of the victim's heart. Conceivably the defendant's lawyers could argue that the victim died, not when his brain ceased to function, but later that day when surgeons removed his heart, which was not actually beating but was "faintly quivering," according to Dr. Cooley. This raised the question, "Was Clarence Nicks killed in the fight or murdered by the physician who removed his heart? Or more confounding, was Nicks alive since his heart was beating inside Stuchwish? Was Stuchwish, whose heart had been removed and disposed of, really dead?"

How would you judge this case? Fortunately, the Cooley medical team that performed the transplant had obtained permission to remove the heart from county medical officers and were therefore not liable for "hiding" or "destroying" evidence.

CONCLUSION

We have examined the terminal phase of life from the moment a person is defined as terminal to the moment she or he dies. Both the behavior of the medical staff and the needs and emotional experiences of the dying have been discussed in considerable detail. In addition, questions surrounding the issue of euthanasia have been raised. Within each of these areas there exist widely divergent views and only limited data are at present available on most questions. Future research should provide some additional answers, but some questions will undoubtedly never be answered.

One such question, thus far not discussed, is the issue of life after death or as Raymond Moody (1976) puts it, "life after life." Moody attempts to answer the question, What is it like to die? For him the answer is found in numerous protocols collected from individuals who had close calls with death. According to Moody, some of the common experiences reported by such individuals include the following: hearing the news that one has died; feeling peaceful and quiet; hearing noises; going through a dark tunnel; having out-of-body experiences; meeting others; seeing a being of light; and so on. Many of these experiences are imbued with religious overtones and, after having such an experience, individuals typically feel more at peace with themselves and their world. While Moody by no means claims to have proven that there is life after death, he does attach great significance to these reports of near death experiences. He further suggests that our present inability to prove that there is life after death may simply reflect "a limitation of the currently accepted modes of scientific and logical thought."

Viewed from our currently "limited" empirical perspective, the significance of his data are suspect on two counts. First, it can be argued that none of the persons who provided protocols were in fact dead. If we accept brain death as our criterion (for example, a flat EEG lasting 24 hours), none of the people discussed in his book would be defined as having been dead. The most that can be claimed is that Moody's case studies had a close brush with death, which evoked a variety of profound emotional experiences, but it is unlikely that these persons actually "returned from the dead."

A second objection can be raised if we consider the way the data were collected. These data are based on observations similar to those of Kübler-Ross (1969). It is therefore difficult to rule out the possibility that these experiences were in part shaped by the open-ended nature of the data-collection procedures.

More systematic and perhaps less biased data could be collected on this topic, but the question, *"Is there life after death?"* will most likely remain a mystery for quite some time.

5
LENGTHENING LIFE

Psychological variables are now almost universally recognized as important determinants of human longevity, both in the long run and in situations where distance to death is perceived to be relatively short. In part, this is because of the publicity the press has given to research in this area. It is not unusual to find articles in *Newsweek* or *Time* magazines discussing how fear, depression, excitement, or being a certain personality type can end, shorten, or extend life. The formulas for long life frequently found in such articles invariably include suggestions for the type of psychological disposition that is best suited for a long life. But psychological variables are clearly not the only determinants of longevity.

What we eat and drink, how much sleep we get, how long our ancestors lived, and a host of other *biological* and *sociological variables* also affect longevity. Some of the more important biological, sociological, and psychological contributors to longevity are identified in Table 5.1. Although this table indicates the relative importance of each of the contributing factors, it is only a very rough guide for calculating longevity. A more detailed discussion of these variables is presented in this chapter.

This chapter is divided into two parts. The biological determinants of longevity, including heredity, are identified and discussed first. The remainder of the chapter—and major portion of this chapter—is devoted to the social-psychological factors important in human longevity.

BIOLOGICAL FACTORS

In the last two decades, the people of three isolated parts of the world have acquired reputations for being exceptionally long-lived. Researchers (Leaf, 1973 and 1975) have extensively studied the inhabitants of Abkhazia in southern Russia, Hunza in the Karkarom Mountains of Pakistan, and Vilcabamba, which is located in the foothills of the Andes Mountains in Ecuador. Since reliable documentation (birth certificates, baptismal records, etc.) is unavailable for many inhabitants of these areas, estimates of their absolute age are probably exaggerated. As age is a sign of status for individuals in these communities, especially in light of the attention from the numerous

TABLE 5.1 *How Long Will You Live?*

This is a rough guide for calculating your personal longevity. The basic life expectancy for males is age 67 and for females it is age 75. Write down your basic life expectancy. If you are in your 50s or 60s, you should add ten years to the basic figure because you have already proven yourself to be quite durable. If you are over age 60 and active, add another two years.

Basic Life Expectancy   *6 7*

Decide how each item below applies to you and add or subtract the appropriate number of years from your basic life expectancy.

1. Family history

   Add 5 years if 2 or more of your grandparents lived to 80 or beyond.   *5*

   Subtract 4 years if any parent, grandparent, sister, or brother died of heart attack or stroke before 50. Subtract 2 years if anyone died from these diseases before 60. _____

   Subtract 3 years for each case of diabetes, thyroid disorders, breast cancer, cancer of the digestive system, asthma, or chronic bronchitis among parents or grandparents.   *- 3*

2. Marital status

   If you are married, add 4 years. _____

   If you are over 25 and not married, subtract 1 year for every unwedded decade. _____

3. Economic status

   Subtract 2 years if your family income is over $40,000 per year.   *- 2*

   Subtract 3 years if you have been poor for greater part of life. _____

4. Physique

   Subtract one year for every 10 pounds you are overweight. _____

   For each inch your girth measurement exceeds your chest measurement deduct two years. _____

   Add 3 years if you are over 40 and not overweight. _____

5. Exercise

   Regular and moderate (jogging 3 times a week), add 3 years.   *3*

   Regular and vigorous (long distance running 3 times a week), add 5 years. _____

   Subtract 3 years if your job is sedentary. _____

   Add 3 years if it is active. _____

6. Alcohol

   Add 2 years if you are a light drinker (1-3 drinks a day). _____

Subtract 5 to 10 years if you are a heavy drinker (more than 4 drinks per day).

Subtract 1 year if you are a teetotaler.   _– 1_

7. Smoking

Two or more packs of cigarettes per day, subtract 8 years.   _____

One to two packs per day, subtract 4 years.   _____

Less than one pack, subtract 2 years.   _____

Subtract 2 years if you regularly smoke a pipe or cigars.   _____

8. Disposition

Add 2 years if you are a reasoned, practical person.   _2_

Subtract 2 years if you are aggressive, intense, and competitive.   _____

Add 1-5 years if you are basically happy and content with life.   _1_

Subtract 1-5 years if you are often unhappy, worried, and often feel guilty.   _____

9. Education

Less than high school, subtract 2 years.   _____

Four years of school beyond high school, add 1 year.   _____

Five or more years beyond high school, add 3 years.   _3_

10. Environment

If you have lived most of your life in a rural environment, add 4 years.   _4_

Subtract 2 years if you have lived most of your life in an urban environment.   _____

11. Sleep

More than 9 hours a day, subtract 5 years.   _____

12. Temperature

Add 2 years if your home's thermostat is set at no more than 68°F.   _____

13. Health Care

Regular medical check ups and regular dental care, add 3 years.   _____

Frequently ill, subtract 2 years.

scientists who are investigating them, it is not surprising that these individuals' ages increase at dramatic rates.

Miguel Carpio, for example, was identified in 1970 as the oldest living person in Vilcabamba, Ecuador; he claimed to be 121 years old. In

*1974, Carpio was interviewed again and he, as well as the villagers,
claimed he was 132 years old—an increase of 11 years in the intervening
four years. A close scrutiny of the baptismal records of Vilcabamba
revealed that Carpio was probably 110 years old—still a venerable age
but considerably younger than his reported age.*

Exaggerated ages were common in all three of the localities
studied, but there was sufficient documentation to convincingly
demonstrate that the rate of centenarians per 100,000 population was
far in excess of rates reported for the rest of the world. Although based
on small total populations, the rates of centenarians per 100,000
population in these three areas of the world are 39, 63, and 1100 in
Abkhazia, Hunza, and Vilcabamba, respectively. The rate is three per
100,000 in the United States (Leaf, 1975). It is unlikely that these
differences can be completely attributed to distorted records. Moreover, the uniformity of environment and life style in these three areas
makes the unusual longevity of the inhabitants believable. Several
biological factors, common to all three areas, have been identified as
important contributors to longevity. These factors are discussed in
some detail next.

Diet
The diets of the inhabitants of Abkhazia, Hunza, and Vilcabamba do
not meet the nutritional recommendations of the United States
National Academy of Sciences, yet these people are neither
malnourished nor obese. Their caloric intake is considerably lower
than the average for the United States. Aged Abkahzians, for example,
consume approximately 1800 calories per day (Leaf, 1975). This is 600
calories less than the number recommended for males over 55 by the
United States National Academy of Sciences.

The second significant characteristic of the diets in these areas is
the absence of animal fats, which have been linked to heart disease. The
typical diet in all three areas consists of fresh and pickled vegetables,
fruits, bread, cheese, milk, wine, and only occasionally meat. Another
notable characteristic of the food consumed in these isolated areas is the
absence of toxins such as pesticides and heavy metals that are more
commonly found in industrialized areas of the world.

More convincing evidence that controlled caloric and choresterol
intake promotes longevity comes from several systematic and control-

led studies carried out in the United States. Rosenman et al. (1970) and Kannel (1971) convincingly demonstrated that weight and cholesterol levels are significantly correlated with mortality due to heart attacks. In both studies, excess weight and high cholesterol levels were good predictors of cardiovascular disease. The relationship between weight, cholesterol, and mortality is so widely accepted that it regularly appears in recipes for long life.

For example, an article on "How to stay young longer" (Cant, 1974) suggests a diet that will keep weight at a reasonable level and is low in cholesterol and sugars. Similar suggestions are made in an article in *McCall's* (1974) on how to "Eat, drink, and live to a ripe old age."

The best way to determine the effects of diet on human longevity would be to systematically manipulate the diet of several groups of individuals from birth. It would, of course, be unethical to use human beings in such an experiment, but such experiments have been done with animals. Ross and Bras (1975) gave 121 randomly bred rats a choice of three diets that varied only in the proportion of protein and carbohydrates. They found a strong correlation between how much the rats ate and how long they lived. Length of life was inversely related to the amount of food consumed. The average life of a rat is approximately 617 days. The rats in the study lived anywhere from 317 to 1026 days. Holding amount of food consumed constant, a low protein diet early in life was more likely to lead to a shortened life span than a high protein diet. Many of the short-lived rats attempted to compensate for the early protein deprivation by eating more protein late in life, but this was unsuccessful. The rats who chose a high protein diet early in life and reduced their protein intake later in life lived longest. Kostolansky (1973) reported results similar to those of Ross and Bras. Although it is often hazardous to generalize from animals to man, the results from the animal studies are compelling in their consistency with available human data.

Several researchers have proposed an anti-aging cocktail in the form of mega-vitamin treatment. Linus Pauling (1974) has long argued that Vitamins C and E can at least indirectly be valuable in prolonging life. According to Pauling, Vitamin C taken in large doses (one to two grams per day) will prevent illnesses such as the common cold and Vitamin E can be useful in preventing arteriosclerosis and heart disease.

Galston (1975) has also suggested that Vitamin E may contribute to longevity in that it may ameliorate the harmful effects of high doses of radiation. Radiation is known to cause the formation of highly reactive *free radicals*, which are molecules with unpaired electrons. "The harmful effect of radiation may result from the modification of nucleic acid and other important molecules by radiation-induced free radicals. One way to get around this trouble is to feed the body compounds that are known as *reducing agents*, or antioxidants. The theory is that such ingested substances will react directly with the free radicals, thus keeping them from affecting important molecules in the cell. Vitamin E, a known antioxidant, has shown some promise in this regard." At present, the effectiveness of mega-vitamin therapy is still being debated. We must wait for future research to discover whether they really can serve as an anti-aging cocktail.

In sum, the available data consistently show that human beings are, in a very real sense, capable of "digging their graves with their teeth" (Senator William Proxmire, 1973). What we eat, when in our development we eat it, and how much of it we eat are all important determinants of longevity.

Alcohol and cigarettes

Moderate amounts of alcohol are consumed by the inhabitants of Vilcabamba, Abkhazia, and Hunza. Cigarette smoking is rare, however. Some of the long-lived residents of Vilcabamba occasionally smoke cigars.

Recent research has shown that in regard to alcohol consumption, the spartan life does not necessarily lead to the longest life. Breslow and Belloc (Kasindorf, 1974) of the California Department of Health selected a cross section of 7000 adults in the Berkeley-Oakland area and studied these adults for five and a half years. They found that the odds *against* an early death were greater for nonsmokers and moderate alcohol drinkers. The survey revealed that the mortality rate for nondrinkers was no better than for those who had up to four drinks per day. Furthermore, individuals who had one or two drinks a day had the longest life expectancy.

Smoking, even in moderate amounts (half a pack a day), caused an increase in sickness and mortality rates and the mortality rates rose steadily as the number of cigarettes per day increased. This result has been replicated by numerous other researchers (Bartko, Patterson, and Butler, 1971; Palmore, 1971a; Kannel, 1971). Bartko, Patterson, and Butler (1971) in their 11-year study of 47 men over 65 years of age found that nonsmokers lived significantly longer than smokers. Palmore (1971a) found that use of tobacco was one of the five strongest predictors of longevity when the factors of age, sex, and race were held constant. Taken together, the available data show that cigarette smoking is directly related to a shortened life-span.

Exercise, rest, and sleep

The most salient characteristic of the long-lived inhabitants of Abkhazia, Vilcabamba, and Hunza is the extent to which they engage in strenuous and sustained physical activity from childhood to very old age. Retirement is unknown to these old persons. In Abkhazia, for example, daily hikes, swimming, and even horseback riding are common among the very old. In all three areas, the steep mountainous terrain in addition to the normal physical demands of farming require a great deal of physical exertion and account for the inhabitants' high degree of cardiovascular fitness.

This is why Leaf (1975) stresses that regular, frequent, and continuous exercise throughout life—rather than speed or strength—is important for longevity. Regular, vigorous exercise improves circulation, reduces heart rate, and speeds the build-up of new bone tissue, which strengthens the bones. Consequently, bone fractures even among the very old were very rare among the long-lived inhabitants of Abkhazia, Vilcabamba, and Hunza. The importance of exercise for long life has been repeatedly documented in the United States (Palmore, 1971a; Friedman and Rosenman, 1974; Kannel, 1971; Proxmire, 1973). Norman Ford calls abundant regular exercise the closest thing to an anti-aging pill. In Proxmire's book *You Can Do It!*, Senator Proxmire advises that a few months of jogging will make you feel better than you ever have in your life and that a year of serious jogging should put you in better condition than some players in the National Football League.

With increasing age, large amounts of sleep become less important. Leaf's (1975) elderly subjects averaged less than eight hours of sleep per day. In the United States, Kasindorf (1974) reported that of the 7000 adults studied in the Berkeley-Oakland area, those who averaged between 7 and 8 hours of sleep a night lived longest.

Environment

Two of the early explanations given for the longevity of Vilcabambans, Hunzakites, and Abkhazians were the high altitudes and the purity of the air in their mountainous environments. It was thought that adaptation of the cardiovascular system to the high altitudes contributed significantly to longevity. The evidence argues against this for the following two reasons: First, the altitude of Abkhazia ranges from 2000 to 6000 feet above sea level, and such altitudes require very minimal adaptation, if any. Second, the villages near Vilcabamba, which are located at similar altitudes and whose inhabitants have somewhat different life styles, do not boast the high number of long-lived individuals found in Vilcabamba. Purity of air may be a factor, but it is unlikely to be a strong positive factor in unusual longevity, although polluted environments undoubtedly have negative effects and may contribute to unusually short life-spans in industrialized environments.

Temperature has also been suggested as a reason for unusual longevity. Although the wide temperature range in Abkhazia and Hunza argues against this explanation, research with subhuman organisms suggests that environmental temperature may indeed be an important factor in longevity. The temperature at which young are raised, particularly with organisms whose body temperatures are not stable, has a significant effect on longevity. For example, fruit flies live ten times longer at 10°C than they do at 30°C. The life span of vertebrates such as fish is increased in cold lakes.

Although little is known about the effect of decreased body temperatures on the nervous system of humans, Strehler (1973) has hypothesized that a decrease in core temperature of 2° to 3°C is unlikely to have noticeably adverse effects and could increase longevity by 20 to 30 years. How this could be accomplished is a question in need of further research. In general, the available data suggest that the rate of aging is reduced in colder environments; as a result, humans may benefit slightly by living in a moderately cool environment.

Heredity

Although there is no known longevity gene, there are "bad" genes, which may increase the probability of contracting a fatal illness. It has been suggested that the unusual longevity of the Vilcabambans and Hunzakites can be attributed to the absence of such bad genes in their forebears. Given the isolation of these areas, it is possible that the inbreeding of persons who lacked "bad" genes accounts for the number of long-lived individuals. This is less likely to be the case in Abkhazia, where centenarians who represent several different ethnic backgrounds including Russians, Georgians, Armenians, Georgian Jews, and Turks can be found. Nevertheless, long-lived persons in all three remote areas generally have long-lived parents and long-lived close relatives.

The importance of the genetic influence on longevity was indicated in a study carried out by Pearl (in Galston, 1975) several decades ago. Pearl showed a positive correlation between parents' and children's ages at death. Forty-six percent of the children who lived beyond age seventy had parents who did likewise; only 13 percent of those reaching 70 had two short-lived parents. Rose (1964) in his study of Spanish-American War Veterans found that his population of octogenarians had longer-lived parents than the population in general. Parental longevity contributes to the longevity of the offspring in two ways. First, there is undoubtedly a hereditary factor, which determines susceptibility to various diseases in the offspring. Second, long-lived parents are more likely to provide a good fostering environment for their children. In the absence of planned human genetic experiments, it is difficult to separate the environmental from the purely genetic determinants of longevity. Experiments with lower organisms, however, have repeatedly demonstrated that life span can be controlled over a wide range through planned genetic selection.

SOCIAL PSYCHOLOGICAL FACTORS

The pattern of life in the three primitive communities of Abkhazia, Vilcabamba, and Hunza changes very little from day to day—they work, eat, sleep, and procreate. Like individuals in the rest of the world, the most important feature of their lives is work, but there is a difference. Many of the stresses and competitive aspects of work in industrialized societies are absent. Psychological well-being in these primitive communities is largely dependent on the individual's ability to contribute to the sustenance of the family. When physical capabilities diminish and some farming chores become impossible, the aged often complain but typically adjust to performing less arduous tasks such as spinning, knitting, chafing, picking coffee, etc.

In addition to the absence of many work-related stressors, two positive psychological factors have been identified as contributors to longevity. First, individuals in these communities *expect* to live a long time. Old age is defined as 100 years old and most expect to reach this age. Second, increased age brings increased prestige. The aged are respected by younger persons and are perceived as necessary and useful members of society. In an environment where little change occurs in the lifetime of an individual, the old become a valuable reservoir of knowledge and skills.

The evidence for respect in old age, expectations for longevity, and importance of stress presented thus far is only anecdotal. Systematic and controlled research carried out in the last three decades supports the relevance of these variables to longevity, and suggests several additional factors. This literature is discussed next.

Stress and the ability to make adjustments

The way in which individuals react to stress has important consequences for their survival. The common belief that prolonged stress can make people sick or even kill them has been substantially proven. Sufficient evidence exists to support the claim that human longevity is affected by both the intensity and duration of the stress experienced, as well as the individual's coping ability.

The discussion that follows is divided into four parts. In the first part, stress is defined and its effects on longevity are demonstrated. Next some specific coping mechanisms that tend to alleviate or intensify the impact of stress are examined. And finally, the psychological and physiological mechanisms mediating between the stressor and its gross observable consequences are examined.

Defining stress Hans Selye (1950), one of the early stress researchers, defined a *stress response* as a nonspecific reaction pattern elicited by a wide range of stimuli that interfere with homeostasis. The initial reaction to a stressor is alarm, which is followed by the instantaneous rallying of the body's defenses—the endocrine glands, particularly the adrenals, are activated. These organs thrive and enlarge under stress. If the threat recedes or is overcome, stability or homeostasis returns. However, if the attack is prolonged, deterioration occurs as the body's defense system gradually wears down. Selye calls this process the *General Adaptation Syndrome.*

This view of stress is easily applied to situations where the stressor is physical, such as a fresh wound or a broken bone. In response to such physical intrusions, the adrenal and pituitary glands produce hormones, which stimulate protective bodily reactions; the blood either seals off the wound or causes swelling around the break. At the same time, anti-inflammatory hormones prevent the body from reacting so strongly that the reaction causes more harm than the invasion.

The one major problem with Selye's physiological view of stress is that it is practically impossible to define the psychological condition that corresponds to a homeostatic steady state (Janis and Leventhal, 1968). A broader and more acceptable definition of stress was proposed by Janis (1958), who defined a stressful event as "any change in the environment which typically—i.e., in the average person—induces a high degree of emotional tension and interferes with normal patterns of response." Here stress is equated with a broad class of emotional behaviors which include fear, grief, rage, and other negative emotional states elicited by aversive stimulation. It should be noted that although stressors are by definition *aversive stimuli*, they can benefit the organism under some circumstances.

Glass and Singer (1972), for example, point out that food deprivation can lead to adaptive behavior and, hence, the survival of the organism. Another example of the beneficial effects of stress can be found in the animal studies of Lindzey, Lykken, and Winston (1960). They found that rats that were stressed during puphood by electric shock or by having their toes pinched developed into more competent adults than their nonstressed counterparts.

Stress and longevity Evidence linking life stress with decreased length of life is frequently reported in medical, sociological, and psychological literature as well as in the popular press. Reporting on research carried out by Bogdonoff, *Newsweek* (1965), for example, described how induced fear may result in death. Bogdonoff frightened the volunteer participants in his experiment by telling them that they had a severe heart condition. All participants showed severe physiological reactions to this distressing news: blood pressure increased, the heart slowed down, and the strength of heart contractions increased sharply. Bogdonoff speculated that severe emotional shock may cause death by forming either a clot in the coronary artery or by disturbing heart rhythms.

Similarly, in an article entitled, "How recession can kill," *Newsweek* (1970) again pointed to psychological stress as a variable mediating life-death outcomes. The article summarized M.H. Brenner's statistical evidence, which showed an increase in deaths due to heart attacks following economic recessions. These findings could not be explained by the availability of less money for medical care because of recessions. Brenner argued that the stress imposed by economic uncertainty precipitates heart attacks in persons already predisposed by the gradual development of arteriosclerosis. The incidence of ulcers and asthma were also found to be related to gross changes in the economy. Many similar examples can be cited.

Barry (1969) compared the longevity of world champion chess players with that of lesser masters and composers of chess problems, expecting to find that chess champions, like eminent men in other fields, live longer than their nonfamous peers. Of the three groups studied, however, the chess champions had the shortest life span. Again, it appears that the stress induced by intense competition may have resulted in their earlier deaths.

It is commonly believed that stress may cause or aggravate heart disease. This belief is supported by evidence collected by Rahe and Lind (1971), who demonstrated that sudden cardiac death is often preceded by an increase in life stress during the six-month period before death. In the Rahe and Lind study, relatives (usually wives) of those who recently had fatal heart attacks were asked to fill out a Schedule of Recent Events questionnaire. Briefly, this questionnaire asked that the relatives report "new life changes" of the deceased during each three-month interval of the three- to four-year time period before death. Each life change was given a weight that reflected the intensity of the change. Examples of some life events and their weights are presented in Table 5.2. The weighted scoring system was used to calculate the mean number and intensity of the life changes for each individual.

Rahe and Lind found that both the number and intensity of the life changes were significantly greater during the six-month period before death than during any other six-month period in the previous four years. This result is obviously confounded by memory differences: it's easier to remember events that occurred four months ago than four years ago. Yet, the intensity of life changes preceding the heart attacks was greater in this study than were found in another study of heart attack patients who subsequently recovered (Rahe, 1969). These results have been replicated using the retrospective methodology of Rahe and Lind (Rahe, Romo, Bennett, and Siltanen, 1973; Theorell and Rahe, 1971; Rahe and Paasikivi, 1971; Theorell, 1974).

Jenkins (1971) also focused on the cardiac patient in his review of the literature on psychological and social precursors of coronary disease. For example, he cited a study by Kits van Heijningen and

TABLE 5.2   *Some events and their weights from the schedule of recent experience.*

Events	Life-change units
Death of spouse	100
Divorce	73
Death of close family member	63
Marriage	50
Retirement	45
Gain of new family member	39
Son or daughter leaving home	29
Begin or end school	26
Vacation	13

Source: Casey, R. L., M. Masuda, and T. H. Holmes. Quantitative study of recall of life events. *J. of Psychosomatic Research*, 11(1968): 239-247.

Teurniet (1966), which indicated that rejection by a loved one, a setback in work, or loss of prestige frequently preceded the emergence of coronary disease. Similar studies (Kritsikis, Heinemann, and Eitner, 1968; Sales, 1969; Russek, 1962 and 1965; and House, 1975) implicated the prolonged emotional strain associated with job responsibilities as a major contributor to coronary disease. Kritsikis identified 150 men with angina pectoris in a large population of industrial workers and attributed their condition to *nerval-psychic overstrain*, caused by the high output demands of their work. Similarly, Sales (1969) reported how *work overload* was related to coronary disease, and Russek (1962, 1965) implicated workers' inability to carry through tasks for which they felt responsible. House (1975) noted job dissatisfaction and job pressures as contributors to coronary disease.

The level of stress a person experiences is determined not only by environmental events but also by enduring characteristics of the individual. Friedman and Rosenman (1974) and Jenkins (1974) have identified a type of person who exhibits a coronary-prone behavior pattern. People who display this behavior are called *Type A individuals*. In general, Type A individuals are characterized by intense drive, ambition, competitiveness, aggressiveness, restlessness, and the habit of pushing themselves against the clock. *Type B individuals* may be equally serious and just as successful, but they are more easygoing in manner, are seldom impatient, do not feel driven by the clock, are less competitive and preoccupied with achievement, and speak in a more modulated, less staccato style. A more detailed description of these types follows:

Extreme Type A individuals are tremendously hard workers and perfectionists, who are filled with brisk self-confidence, decisiveness, and resolution. They never evade. They are the ones who, while waiting in the cardiologist's or dentist's office, are on the telephone making business calls. Their mates are certain they drive themselves too hard, and they may be a little in awe of these Type A individuals. Life is a deadly serious game, and these individuals are out to amass enough points to win.

Extreme Type A individuals speak in staccato style and have a tendency to end their sentences in a rush. They frequently sigh faintly between words, but never in anxiety because that state is strange to them. They are seldom out sick; they rarely go to doctors and almost never to psychiatrists. They are unlikely to get ulcers. They are rarely interested in money (except as a token of the game), but the higher they climb, the more they consider themselves to be underpaid.

On the debit side, extreme Type A individuals are often a little difficult to get along with. Their laugh is rather grim. They do not drive the people who work under them as hard as they drive themselves, but they have little time to waste with these people. They want their respect, not their affection. Yet, in some ways, they are more sensitive to others than the milder Type B individuals. They hate to fire anyone and will go to great lengths to avoid it. Sometimes the only way they can resolve such situations is by mounting a crisis. If they have ever been fired, it was probably after a personality clash.

Surprisingly, Type A individuals probably go to bed earlier most nights than Type B individuals, who often become interested in matters that are irrelevant to their careers and sit up late, or simply socialize. Type A individuals are precisely on time for appointments and they expect the same treatment from others. They smoke cigarettes, never pipes. Headwaiters learn not to keep Type A individuals waiting for table reservations; if they do, they may lose them as customers. Actually, headwaiters prefer Type A individuals because they don't linger over meals, and they don't complain about quality. They will usually salt the meal before they taste it and they have never sent back a bottle of wine in their lives.

When driving cars, Type A individuals are not reckless, but they do reveal anger when slower drivers delay them. Type A individuals are not much for exercise, claiming that they have too little time for it. If they play golf, it is usually fast through. Their desk tops are clean when they leave the office at the end of each day, and they would never return late from their vacations.

However, when in competition for the top jobs in their organizations, Type A individuals often lose out to Type B individuals because they are too competitive. They are so obsessed with the office that they have little attention for anything else, including their families. They make decisions too quickly—in minutes rather than hours or days—and so make serious business mistakes. They are intoxicated by numerical competition—for example, how many units were sold in Phoenix or how many miles were traveled last month? Also Type A individuals frequently have about them an "existential" miasma of hostility that makes others nervous.

Type B individuals differ little in background or ability from Type A individuals and, although they may be quietly urgent, they are more reasonable individuals. Unlike Type A individuals, Type B individuals are hard to "needle" into anger. Type A individuals have no respect for Type B individuals, but smart Type B individuals use Type A individuals. Great salespeople are A's, while corporation presidents are usually B's (McQuade, 1972).

The incidence of coronary heart disease among Type A individuals is two to three times greater than among Type B individuals. In one study, Friedman and Rosenman (1974) interviewed 3500 males between the ages of 39 and 59 and classified them as either Type A or Type B individuals. A double-blind procedure was used so that the team rating behavior types had no knowledge of other risk factors of coronary disease involved and did not participate in the follow-up diagnosis of the presence or absence of coronary disease. The diagnostic team was blind to the presence of any risk factors or behavior types. The incidence of coronary disease in these previously healthy males was assessed 4½, 6½, and 8½ years later; Type A males had 1.7 to 4.5 times the rate of new coronary disease as males exhibiting the easygoing Type B pattern.

Stressful life events have been implicated as precipitators of not only coronary disease but also fractures, childhood leukemia, various psychiatric disorders (including acute schizophrenia), depression, suicide attempts, neurosis, poor teacher performance, low college grade point averages, and college football players' injuries (Dohrenwend and Dohrenwend, 1974). A recent study by Vinokur and Selzer (1975) showed that an accumulation of life events was positively correlated with behavioral indicators of stress such as drinking and traffic accidents, although this relationship held only for undesirable (e.g., deterioration in working conditions), not desirable (e.g., improvement in working conditions) life events. It appears that both the quality and quantity of life changes are important determinants of individuals' responses to life changes.

Finally, although we know that stressful life events play some role in the development of illness, we do not clearly understand how life events interact with social, psychological, biological, and personality variables. To unravel this interaction, we need to know *"what* events influence *what* illnesses under *what* conditions and through *what* processes"* (Mechanic, 1974). Some probable psychological and physiological mediators of the response to stress are discussed later in this chapter.

Stress and longevity of the aged Some investigators have been able to study the effects of stress on aged individuals by examining those who are subjected to severe environmental changes. Elderly people who are forced to relocate for reasons such as urban renewal, debilitating physical decline, or decreased financial resources are often stressed by the loss of a familiar and supportive environment and by the demands of coping with a new set of stimuli in an unfamiliar setting. The predominant finding is that relocation has negative effects on the elderly. Many researchers (Lieberman, 1961; Aldrich and Mendkoff, 1963; Killian, 1970; Markus, Blenkner, Bloom, and Downs, 1972; and Schulz and Aderman, 1973) have claimed that the psychological and physical well-being of the sick and elderly are adversely affected by abrupt or severe changes in their living environment. The adverse effects are typically assessed by measures of mortality, depression, and activity level.

Both Killian (1970) and Lieberman (1961) reported a relationship between residential change and death. With patients matched for factors such as age, sex, race, health, functional status, length of hospitalization, and ability to ambulate, Killian found that a group of patients transferred from Stockton State Hospital in California to other institutions had a higher death rate than a control group that was allowed to remain at Stockton. In the Lieberman study, the percentage of individuals who died within one year of admission to a home for the aged was compared to the death rate among those individuals waiting to be admitted to the same institution; there were proportionately more deaths among those already admitted.

Kasteler, Gray, and Carruth (1968) and Brand and Smith (1974) used personal adjustment, amount of activity, and life satisfaction as the dependent measures. Their results were consistent with those of Killian and Lieberman. Kasteler et al. compared a sample of aged individuals who were moved because of highway construction with a matched sample of nonrelocated controls. The relocated group scored significantly lower on measures of personal adjustment and amount of activity. Brand and Smith also compared relocatees with nonrelocated controls. The control group scored significantly higher than the relocated group on a life satisfaction index.

Schulz and Aderman (1973) took a slightly different approach to the problem of the effects of environmental change on mortality by studying terminal cancer patients. While most of the previous investigators used mortality rates as a dependent measure, Schulz and Aderman were able to use the length of survival in a cancer institute as their dependent measure since almost all (98 percent) of their subjects died within a relatively short time. The data were collected at the North Carolina Cancer Institute, a state facility providing long-term care for indigent patients with terminal cancer. "Institute" is perhaps a misleading term because it had no facilities for surgery, radiation treatment, or exotic chemotherapy. It was, in short, a place to die.

Schulz and Aderman hypothesized that the time to death would vary as a function of the patients' preadmission living arrangements. They reasoned that those patients who had come to the cancer institute from their homes experienced a more severe environmental change and would therefore die sooner than those who had come to the institute from another institution such as a hospital. The data supported their hypothesis. Those patients who came to the institute from other hospitals survived nearly one month longer (60 vs. 32 days) on the average than the patients who came from a home environment. These data are valid only to the extent that no physical differences existed in the two populations when they entered the cancer institute. That this was the case is supported by information gathered from several sources.

First, the director of the North Carolina Cancer Institute (who was unaware of the hypothesis) stated that he was unaware of any differences in physical deterioration between the two groups of patients at the time of admission. Second, patients coming from home were slightly younger than patients coming from hospitals. Finally, the diagnostic homogeneity of the two populations is attested to by the fact that hardly any of the patients (less than 1 percent of 388 patients) survived for more than nine months.

To argue that degree of environmental change is related to relocation mortality is easy. Explaining more precisely why or how a change in surroundings produces such negative effects is more difficult. Before we examine more closely the psychological processes that mediate the effects of relocation in particular and stress in general, one more psychological variable must be identified as an important determinant of life-death outcomes—that is, the *will to live*.

Hope, hopelessness, and longevity Extensive observational and correlational evidence emphasizes the importance of *hope* in maintaining life and hopelessness in fostering deterioration.

Working with archival data, Phillips (1969) showed how a strong desire or reason for living might lengthen life. He examined the birth and death dates of 1251 famous Americans and found that death occurred *least* often in the month before birthdays and most often in the months *after* birthdays. Attempts to replicate these results with nonfamous Americans have failed. David Aderman and I examined 409 county death certificates in North Carolina and found no systematic relationship between birth date and death date. The difference in results might be explained by the fact that birthdays are more meaningful for famous Americans because their birthdays are often publicized and sometimes celebrated nationwide. Phillips also found that the death rate in cities with large Jewish populations declined the month before Yom Kippur, the high holy Day of Atonement. Even elections have induced people to stay alive long enough to find out the outcome. The death rate declined before every United States presidential election from 1904 to 1964.

In observations of American prisoners of war, Nardini (cited in LeShan, 1961) noted that

where the will to live was for any reason weak, death seemed to come readily even with lesser physical ailments. On the other hand, where the will was firm even in the presence of serious physical illness, life often continued.

The relationship between *hopelessness* and shortened temporal distance to death was also observed by others (Weisman and Hackett, 1961; LeShan, 1961; Beard, 1969; Kimball, 1969; and Kübler-Ross, 1969). Weisman and Hackett (1961), for example, discussed five surgical patients whose physical condition did not indicate imminent death. However, on admission to the hospital, the patients overtly expressed hopelessness about their chances of survival and, contrary to medical prognosis, died shortly after admission. Similarly, Kübler-Ross found that when terminally ill patients no longer anticipated recovery they were likely to die soon afterwards.

Several researchers have suggested that the will to live is especially important to the physical well-being of kidney patients and their adjustment to hemodialysis (Eisendrath, 1969; McKegney and Lange, 1971). Eisendrath (1969) concluded from interviews of chronic renal patients that feelings of depression and hopelessness precede death. In a study of 25 dialysis patients, McKegney and Lange (1971) observed that, for those who died, "hope wanes as the expectation of a transplant, good health, and freedom from dialysis are constantly disappointed." Before their deaths, the nonsurvivors lost all hope, explicitly rejecting the life prescribed by their disease.

Less subjective and more convincing evidence of the relationship between hope and time to death comes from correlational studies of the seriously ill. Paloucek and Graham (cited in LeShan, 1961) attributed the negative response to treatment by some of their patients with cancer of the cervix to hopelessness. They divided their patients into two groups, matched for state of the disease and type of treatment. Members of the first group reported a "miserable childhood, a bitterly unhappy married life, and a bleak, hopeless future," whereas members of the second group reported a happier childhood and marital experiences and were more hopeful about the future. Fifty-seven percent of the first group responded poorly to treatment, but only 15 percent of the second group responded poorly. When asked, all the females in the first group viewed their future as "hopeless or totally unacceptable," while only 15 percent of those in the second group felt this way.

Similar findings were reported by Verwoerdt and Elmore (1967). Of 30 terminally ill patients, the 11 patients who were most hopeless died within two months of the assessment date, whereas another 11 patients lived from one to seven months longer. Physical status, which was assessed at the same time the hope questionnaires were administered, had no relation to time of death. Kastenbaum and Kastenbaum (1971) found that patients rated by the medical staff as having a high level of *will to die* tended to die sooner than predicted from medical status alone, but that level of will to live was not related to survival. The Kastenbaums attributed the lack of strong findings to the tendency of the medical staff to make unrealistic judgments of favorable prognosis.

Two issues are raised by the extensive literature linking stress and hopelessness with decreased longevity and hope with increased longevity. One is *methodological* and the other is *theoretical*; both are examined in some detail.

Methodological issues Problems in both the research techniques and the design of these studies leave the important question of *causality* unanswered. It is not clear, for example, whether hope affects the course of illness, or conversely. Or, it may be that the medical staff somehow becomes aware of the patient's prognosis and conveys this information to her or him; the patient in turn becomes hopeless as a consequence of her or his awareness of impending demise.

Similar problems are encountered when the data linking stressful life events with decreased longevity are examined. Since correlational findings seldom explain relationships, alternative explanations can be easily generated for much of the reported data. In addition, problems with assessment techniques magnify interpretive difficulties; too often, data collection techniques (e.g., personal observations, nonblind interviews) threaten validity and reliability. Research techniques, such as experimental studies, are useful in ruling out alternative explanations and in testing causal models for correlational findings, but these techniques are rarely used in applied settings.

Not only do experimental procedures frequently provide less ambiguous answers to research questions, but they also serve as useful pedagogical devices as well. They require an operational version of the theoretical construct and this demands a clear understanding of the *construct*. Take either the construct *hope* or *hopelessness* as an example. Both the lay public and researchers who are interested in death and dying frequently use these words. We usually assume that the meaning of these constructs is self-evident. Yet, when asked how one would go about increasing or decreasing a person's level of hope or hopelessness, we often become at least momentarily tongue-tied while we search for an answer that is often difficult to find.

Operationalizing a construct is a process very much like this. It forces the researcher to generate operations designed to eliminate or induce a particular state. One major consequence of this process is that the construct is often more clearly understood even before the experiment is carried out. Assuming that the experiment is carefully planned and executed, we should gain not only accurate descriptions, but also an understanding of human beings as they interact with their world. In the following section, we will attempt to understand constructs such as hope and hopelessness, and some of the descriptive relationships between stress, illness, and mortality.

Conceptual issues Earlier, we argued strongly that certain types of events (e.g., traumatic incident, environmental change, a birthday) directly affect longevity. We further implied that the effects of these environmental events were mediated by some specific psychological processes. Although a large number of events were discussed, we argued that a few psychological processes can account for most of the observed relationships. A process common to all these relationships will be derived after examining each in some detail.

Many researchers have used the words hope and hopelessness, but ew have attempted to clearly specify what they mean. Dictionary definitions distinguish between hope as a noun and hope as a verb. When used as a noun, hope is defined as "a wish or desire supported by some confidence of its fulfillment." As a verb, hope means "to entertain a wish for something with some expectation" or "to look forward to with confidence of fulfillment; expect with desire" (*American Heritage Dictionary*, 1970). Psychologists are interested in the latter usage. Several researchers have focused on the individual's perceived probability of certain events as determinants of hope. Kastenbaum and Kastenbaum (1971) describe hope as a *psychic or phenomenological state*, pointed toward the future with a predominantly positive affective glow—a view very similar to the dictionary definition, "expect with desire."

Furthermore, hope exists only if there is an element of uncertainty or suspense present—that is, one hopes only if the subjective probability of an event is greater than 0 percent and less than 100 percent. Hope and expectation are not synonymous. An individual may have expectations for particular outcomes, but an expectation with no affect associated with it is merely an expectancy and not hope. Stotland (1969) and Melges and Bowlby (1969) generally propose that the higher the perceived probability of attaining a goal and the greater the importance of that goal, the higher the level of hope, and the greater the positive affect.

The existing definitions of hope and related concepts focus primarily on the perceived probability of specific events. Columns 2 and 3 of Table 5.3 indicate, for example, that hope is high when the perceived probability of a good event is high or the perceived probability of a bad event is low. That is, one can hope for something good to happen or for something bad *not* to happen. However, as depicted in Columns 4 and 5 of Table 5.3, hope can also be viewed as a general phenomenological state—that is, dependent on the individual's perceived effectiveness in controlling his or her future outcomes. Thus individuals are hopeful when they perceive themselves to be generally in control of their future outcomes and perceive others to have relatively little control over their outcomes. In short, they view themselves as masters of their fate. This definition of hope differs from Rotter's (1960) concept of internal control in that hope is viewed as a transient state that comes and goes as a function of the individual's experiences with her or his environment, rather than as a personal disposition.

If hopelessness is the opposite of hope, then it should follow that the organism is hopeless when the perceived probability of positive events is low or the perceived probability of negative events is high.

TABLE 5.3 *Differentiation of hope and related terms.*

| | Perceived probability of positive or negative event | | Perceived effectiveness of self and others in determining outcomes for self | | Affective state |
	Positive event	Negative event	Self's control of future outcomes	Others' control of future outcomes	
Hope	High	Low	High	Low	Positive glow
Dread	Low	High	Low	High	Anxiety
Helplessness	Low	Low	Low	High	Depression
Hopelessness	Low	Low	Low	Low	Extreme depression

Source: Schulz, R. Some life and death consequences of perceived control. J. Carroll and J. Payne (eds.), *Cognition and Social Behavior*, New York: Erlbaum, 1976. Reprinted by permission.

However, Kastenbaum and Kastenbaum (1971) call this *dread*. An individual dreads the anticipated absence of a positive outcome and the anticipated presence of a negative outcome. A generalized state of dread may result when individuals feel that others control their future outcomes rather than themselves. The affective state associated with dread is *anxiety* (see Table 5.3).

In contrast, the hopeless person does not believe that outcomes are contingent on his or her behavior nor does he or she believe that anyone else can provide meaningful outcomes for him or her. The hopeless individual perceives the probabilities of either positive or negative events as low, and the associated affective state is extreme depression and psychological and physical withdrawal (Seligman, 1975). As LeShan (1961) puts it, the hopeless person lacks the belief that outside objects can bring any satisfaction, has no faith in development or the possibility of change, and does not believe that any action he or she or anyone else may take can ease his or her aloneness.

Closely related to the concept of hopelessness is *helplessness*. As Table 5.3 indicates, the helpless individual feels incapable of controlling her or his own outcomes, but perceives the possibility of others providing outcomes for her or him.

These definitions of hope and the related concepts of dread, hopelessness, and helplessness focus on the following two issues: (1) the perceived probability of good and bad events, and (2) beliefs about control over the environment exercised by the individual relative to others in his or her environment. This latter issue becomes increasingly important because of the convergent evidence in other areas of experimental psychology on the importance of *control* and *predictability* as mediators of an organism's physical and psychological functioning. Before examining this evidence, we will return to the findings on stress and environmental change and attempt to more thoroughly understand the psychological processes operating here.

Relocation is a major change in the lives of most individuals. Like other important life events, relocation can be stressful and may exact a price both psychologically and physically from the person who experiences this change. Gutman and Herbert (1976) suggest that the chances of death from relocation are related to the degree of environmental change, independent of transfer procedure and the individual characteristics of the relocated persons.

The relocation literature can be readily classified on two dimensions: the degree of choice the persons have in deciding to move and the degree of environmental change they experience as a result of the move (Schulz and Brenner, 1977). Three types of environmental change can be identified: (1) institution to institution, (2) home to institution, and (3) home to home. Schulz and Brenner (1977) reviewed the extensive relocation literature and argued that, holding other things constant, the effects of relocation are least negative (or most positive) when an individual is relocated voluntarily and when the degree of environmental change is minimized. Thus, individuals moved involuntarily from one setting to a *dissimilar* setting (home to institution) showed the greatest negative effects, with the outcomes being somewhat better for involuntary relocatees moved from one setting to a similar setting (home to home or institution to institution). Finally, the outcomes of individuals moving voluntarily from institution to institution or home to home were found to be least negative when compared to the other groups.

Another way of viewing the voluntary-involuntary dimension in relocation is in terms of *control*. Having a choice is equivalent to being able to control one's outcomes. The environmental change dimension translates directly into *predictability*. The less severe the change, the more the individual can predict how the new environment will be, and the greater the preparation for a move, the greater the predictability. Applying these concepts to a specific case described earlier, we argue that the adverse reactions (i.e., dying soon after admission) of terminal cancer patients moved from home to the institution is mediated by feelings of helplessness and that such feelings are aroused to the extent that the patients perceived the institutional demands for passivity as a loss in their ability to control their environment. Those patients who came from other hospitals undoubtedly did not exercise as much control over their former environments as did the patients who came from home. Consequently, they suffered less from feelings of helplessness upon entering the Cancer Institute than did patients moved from home.

Relocation is only one type of stressful life event. The effects on health of events ranging in seriousness from the death of a spouse to getting a low grade on an exam appear to be mediated by their predictability and controllability. Elaine Shelton and I (Schulz and Shelton, 1976) recently asked a group of students to keep diaries listing all meaningful events, how predictable and controllable they were, and all physical illness symptons they experienced over a two-month period. The correlation between number of days ill and total number of life events was +0.69—that is, the greater the number of events, the more sick days the person experienced. When the life events were separated into controllable and uncontrollable life events, the correlation between number of days ill and type of events was +0.53 and +0.77 for controllable and uncontrollable events, respectively. Similar results were obtained for predictable and unpredictable events. These data show that uncontrollable and unpredictable events have a greater negative impact than controllable or predictable events. Extensive experimental research with both animals and humans further supports the notion that controllability and predictability are the important mediators of an organism's response to stress.

In his recent review of the experimental control literature, Averill (1973) distinguishes three types of personal control—behavioral, cognitive, and decisional—and points out that each can be beneficial in alleviating the negative effects of a stressor. *Behavioral control* is defined as "the availability of a response which may directly influence or modify the objective characteristics of a threatening event" and involves behaviors such as determining who administers a noxious stimulus and how and when the stimulus will be encountered. Findings from the existing research (e.g., Pervin, 1963; Ball and Volger, 1971; Staub, Tursky, and Schwartz, 1971) indicate that behavioral control reduces stress by reducing the uncertainty about the nature and/or timing of a threatening event. Implicit uncertainty is reduced when predictability is increased.

While behavioral control involves direct action on the environment, cognitive control refers to the way in which a potentially harmful event is interpreted. Specifically, *cognitive control* is defined as "the processing of potentially threatening information in such a manner as to reduce the net long-term stress and/or psychic cost of adaptation" (Averill, 1973). A simple example of this type of control is the case where a warning signal precedes the onset of an aversive stimulus. According to Seligman (1975) and Weiss (1970), a warning signal lessens stress because the subject learns not only that the warning signal precedes an aversive stimulus, but also that the absence of the signal predicts safety.

Decisional control is usually operationalized as the range of choices or number of options open to an individual. For example, Corah and Boffa (1970) studied decisional control by giving subjects the choice of avoiding or not avoiding the aversive consequences of a stimulus. Subjects given a choice experienced less stress both in terms of subjective self-report and automatic arousal than did a no-choice group.

On a broader scale, Schulz (1976b) and Seligman (1975) have emphasized the importance of control for the normal psycho-social development of organisms from infancy to old age. More specifically, Schulz (1976a) hypothesized that some of the characteristics frequently observed among the aged, such as feelings of depression and helplessness, as well as accelerated physical decline, are in part attributable to loss of control. A field experiment in which the institutionalized elderly were randomly assigned to one of four conditions was carried out to assess the effects of increased control and predictability upon the physical and psychological well-being of the aged. The individuals in three of the four conditions were visited by college undergraduates under varying contingencies, while persons in the fourth condition were not visited and served as a baseline comparison group. Subjects in the control condition could determine both the frequency and duration of the visits they received. To assess the effects of predictability, a second group of subjects (predict) was informed when they would be visited and how long the visitor would stay, but had no control over these details. A third group (random condition) was visited on a random schedule. Holding the amount of visitation and the quality of the interaction constant across the three groups, strong support was found for the hypothesis that predictable and controllable positive events have a powerful positive impact upon the well-being of the institutionalized aged.

While it is clear that predictability and control are important psychological variables related to longevity, the available experimental research raises several questions of both theoretical and practical significance:

1 To what extent is predictability itself beneficial, independent of control? And, is having control beneficial above and beyond predictability or can all the effects of control be accounted for by the predictability component of control? The completed research does not clearly differentiate these variables at the operational level, leaving questions about the relative importance of each unanswered.

2   Existing laboratory research suggests that lack of control is most devastating when it has broad implications for the individual's self-worth. To what extent are the effects of control mediated by feelings of increased competence?

3   Finally, we know little about how control and predictability affect the individual. To construct a model that would enable us to predict the impact of these variables at any given point in a person's life, we need data on individual differences. A person's experiences with control and prediction probably contribute greatly to his or her expectancies for a controllable and predictable world, and his or her response to a particular environment is probably affected by the degree to which these expectancies are met.

Thus far, we have identified lack of control and predictability as a possible psychological mediator between a stressor and the ensuing negative consequences (e.g., shortened temporal distance to death). How can a psychological mediator influence physiological processes? Several animal researchers have addressed this question. Curt Richter (1957), in a series of studies using wild and domesticated rats, demonstrated the direct physiological consequences of feelings of hopelessness. Richter observed that wild rats held in such a way as to abolish all hope of escape subsequently died after immersion in water-filled jars from which escape was impossible. Domesticated rats who were used to being handled rarely died in this situation. Richter interpreted the sudden death of wild rats as the result of feelings of hopelessness; this was supported by a subsequent study showing that when feelings of hopelessness are eliminated, the rats do not die. He did this by repeatedly holding the wild rats and then releasing them and by occasionally immersing them in water for a few minutes. "In this way," stated Richter, "rats quickly learn that the situation is not actually hopeless; thereafter they again become aggressive, try to escape, and show no signs of giving up. Wild rats so conditioned swim just as long as domesticated rats or longer."

Electrocardiographic (EKG) records indicated that the cause of death in hopeless rats was the slowing of the heart rate rather than acceleration, as expected on the basis of Cannon's (1942) speculations on the importance of the sympathetic nervous system in emotional states. Autopsies of the animals corroborated the EKG record, revealing large hearts distended with blood. These findings led Richter to conclude that the rats died as a result of overstimulation of the parasympathetic system rather than the sympathetic system. This conclusion is supported by two additional findings:

1   Domesticated rats that were injected with sublethal amounts of cholinergic drugs, which stimulate the parasympathetic system, died within a few minutes after being placed in the swimming jars, just as the wild rats did.

2   Adrenalectomized wild rats still showed the sudden-death response, indicating that the deaths were not due to an overwhelming supply of adrenalin produced by the sympathetic system.

Richter drew a parallel between the wild rats who died in his water jars and primitive men and voodoo death. The "boned victim, like the wild rat, is not set for fight or flight, but similarly seems resigned to his fate—his situation seems to him quite hopeless." Richter suggested that even in our own culture, cases of unexplained sudden death might be the result of intense feelings of hopelessness and the accompanying physiological overstimulation of the parasympathetic system.

The direct physiological consequences of helplessness were again demonstrated by Jay Weiss (1970, 1971, 1972) and Robert Ader (1971) in a series of rat studies. In the first study of this series (1970), Weiss showed that a predictable stressor significantly reduced the amount of gastric ulceration in rats. The rats were randomly assigned to one of three groups:

1   The stress-predictable group—these animals heard a beep before being shocked.

2   The stress-not-predictable group—these animals heard a random beep and were exposed to electric shock.

3   A control group—these animals received no shocks.

Animals in the control group showed little or no gastric ulceration as did animals in the stress-predictable group, while the stress not-predictable animals showed considerable ulceration. In two follow-up studies (Weiss, 1971; Ader, 1971), one group of rats was able to avoid or escape the shock by jumping onto a platform. These animals were yoked to "partners," who received the same number of and intensity shocks, but had no opportunity to escape. In the first follow-up study (Weiss, 1971), the yoked rats lost significantly more weight than the avoidance-escape rats. In the second follow-up study (Ader, 1971), extent of gastric ulcerations was the dependent measure, and the yoked animals had an average of 4.5 millimeters of lesion while the escape-avoidance rats had only 1.6 millimeters of lesion.

Perhaps of even greater significance is the association between catecholamine levels in the central nervous system and psychological state. Rats able to avoid and escape shock showed an increase in the level of brain norepinephrine, whereas helpless animals showed a decrease in norepinephrine. High levels of norepinephrine are thought to be important in mediating active, assertive responses, while depletion of norepinephrine is viewed by some (see Schildkraut and Kety, 1967; Coppen, 1968) as a factor in depression in humans. Weiss (1972) speculated,

It may well be that the causal sequence leading from helplessness to behavioral depression depends on biochemical changes in the central nervous system such as changes in norepinephrine. This would indicate that depressed behavior can be perpetuated in a vicious circle—the inability to cope alters neural biochemistry, which further accentuates depression, increasing the inability to cope, which further alters neural biochemistry, and so on.

Social determinants

Social class and marital status are two important predictors of longevity. Married persons have a greater life expectancy than persons who are not married. Individuals with high social status—as measured by occupation, income, and education—live longer than low social status persons.

Rose (1964), Rose and Bell (1971), Palmore (1971b), and Pfeiffer (1971) have found a positive relationship between occupation, income, education, and length of life. In a study of 149 octogenarian Spanish American War Veterans, Rose (1964) evaluated the social and demographic norms. The octogenarians had a median intelligence quotient of 110 on the Wechsler Adult Intelligence Scale, a higher proportion of high school graduates than their deceased peers, and higher occupational status with 68 percent ranked in the skilled, white collar, and higher categories. Pfeiffer (1971), in his investigation of aged volunteers in the Duke Longitudinal Study on Aging, found similar results. Persons who were highly intelligent and had sound financial status lived significantly longer than their less intelligent and poorer peers.

How does social class affect longevity? Rose (1971) reasoned that higher intelligence leads to more education which, in turn, facilitates attainment of higher status jobs; higher status jobs pay more and are usually less hazardous. Persons with lower status jobs, on the other hand, are more prone to occupational hazards such as "fatigue, inorganic dust (notably silica and asbestos), absorption of poison, excessive heat, and sudden variations in temperature and dampness." Higher status positions also have more liberal sick leave benefits, which make it unnecessary for the worker to stay on the job when he or she should be home nursing his or her health. The more educated are also more likely to be aware of the importance of maintaining their health and the availability of health-maintaining resources. The causal chain depicted by this reasoning begins with intelligence and ends with increased life span.

As shown in Figure 5.1, the relationship between intelligence and longevity is probably mediated by several intervening factors such as education and job status. Of course, this social model is only speculative. It is possible that intelligence and longevity are the result of a common genetic antecedent, in addition to or instead of being causally related.

Intelligence ⟶ Education ⟶ Job status ⟶ Longevity

FIG. 5.1   One possible model explaining the
                                relationship between intelligence
                                and longevity.

For example, an early study by the Metropolitan Life Insurance Company (1932) showed that graduates of eight eastern colleges had a higher life expectancy than the general white male population. However, males who graduated with honor had an even better life expectancy. If we assume that these individuals were an especially intelligent group, these data suggest that intelligence is directly linked to longevity. Another study by the Metropolitan Life Insurance Company (1968) showed that distinguished professional and business men, who were listed in *Who's Who* had superior longevity. For all ages studied (45 to 64), the mortality rate of the *Who's Who* group was below that of the general population and below that of the general white population in similar occupations. These findings again suggest that intelligence and longevity are directly linked.

Like social class, marital status has consistently been found to be a predictor of longevity. Except for females between the ages of 20 and 24 (reflecting the risks of pregnancy), married persons of both sexes and all ages have a longer life expectancy than their single counterparts. The longer life expectancy of married individuals can be attributed to an interaction of biological and social factors. On the one hand, those in poor health and having an unfavorable temperament would choose not to marry or would not have the opportunity to marry. Those who do marry, on the other hand, would not only be more healthy because of selection processes, but would also benefit from the emotional support, better nutrition, and loving care provided by the spouse in time of illness. Even a nagging spouse, who might be very stressful, can aid longevity by helping the husband or wife to remember medical checkups, to drive more safely, to avoid physically risky situations, and so on.

Cognitive functioning

We have already noted that intelligence interacts with social variables such as education and occupation to increase longevity. Some evidence relates general cognitive functioning to lengthened life, even when there is no variation in social class. Bartko, Patterson, and Butler (1971) studied 47 aged males at five-year intervals from 1955 to 1966. At the end of eleven years, 23 were still alive and 24 had died. For each subject, data pertaining to 600 variables were collected and analyzed by multivariate analysis. Two cognitive variables, mental status and the degree of organization of behavior, were significantly related to survival. Subjects with high scores on either variable were more likely to be alive at the end of the 11-year period.

Mental status was a measure of the degree of organic mental decline plus life-long intelligence, and organization of behavior reflected "the level of planning, complexity, and variation characteristic of the men's daily lives." A five-point scale ranging from "activities are few; these are chores, routines, as necessity requires, and little variation" to "many activities; structured, planned, varied, involved, new, complex, and self-initiated" was used to assess organization of behavior. It is easy to see that this scale measures not only the subject's cognitive functioning, but also his or her social and emotional state; one suspects that it predicts well largely because it is so broad. Nevertheless, the data did indicate that *cognitive and emotional involvement in living is beneficial to survival.*

In an almost identical study, Lieberman (1971) found cognitive functioning a significant predictor of survival among 200 aged individuals who were studied over a two-year period. Cognitive functioning was broadly defined as the weighted sum of scores on seven psychological tests, ranging from the paired-word association learning test to time judgments of 30- and 60-second intervals to Murray TAT card responses.

These studies show that absolute differences in cognitive functioning, though broadly defined, are predictive of death and survival. Kleemeier (1961, 1962) has, in addition, suggested that the *rate of decline* in cognitive ability is an important predictor of longevity.

Studying a small group of elderly patients, Kleemeier (1962) found that four of his thirteen subjects showed a rapid decline in menatl ability (measured by the Wechsler Bellevue Intelligence Scale) in the last two years of his four-year longitudinal study; he found no differences in cognitive ability in the first two years. The four men who declined were the first to die. Kleemeier reasoned "that factors related to the death of the individual cause a decline in intellectual performance, and that the onset of this decline may be detected in some instances several years prior to the death of the person."

Thus changes in cognitive ability may be a delicate source of cues for detecting the aging process and the approaching breakdown of vital functions.

In a subsequent study, Kleemeier (1962) replicated his previous findings, showing that the annual rate of performance decline on intelligence tests was much lower for survivors than for subjects who died. This finding has been consistently replicated by other researchers, including Goldfarb (1969), Berkowitz (1965), Lieberman (1965), and Riegel (1971). Riegel called the sudden decline in cognitive ability before death the *terminal drop.*

The consistency of the available evidence warrants some confidence in the conclusion that cognitive ability is positively correlated with life span. This implies a genetic factor linked to intelligence as a primary basis for the length of life. One way of testing this view, suggests Granick (1971), is to follow the intellectually gifted children studied by Terman and Oden (1959) into middle and old age.

This would go a long way toward clarifying the extent to which cognition, combined with other factors, could be used to predict life span. It could also contribute significantly to our understanding of the genetic relationship between longevity and cognitive endowment.

Role and life satisfaction

"Happiness—The Best Preventive Medicine" is the title of a recent (1976) *Reader's Digest* article. In this article, Blake Clark stresses a cheerful disposition and contentment with life as important characteristics of America's centenarians. Although these conclusions are based on anecdotal data, more systematic research also suggests that "songs and laughter somehow lubricate the biological clock and keep it running longer."

As part of the Duke Longitudinal Study of Aging, Palmore (1971b) assessed work satisfaction and general happiness as possible predictors of longevity. The volunteer subjects, initially 60 to 94 years of age, were asked to agree or disagree with statements such as, "I am happy only when I have definite work to do," "I am satisfied with the work I now do," "I can no longer do any kind of useful work, I have no work to look forward to."

Happiness was assessed by a social worker who rated each subject on a zero to nine scale ranging from "unhappy, discontented, worried, and fearful" to "very happy, exultant, and great contentment." In a 15-year follow-up, both work satisfaction and happiness were significant predictors of length of life, when age was controlled. Those participants with greater work satisfaction and higher happiness ratings lived significantly longer. From these findings, Palmore concluded that some important ways to live longer may be to maintain a useful and satisfying role in society, and a positive view of life.

In what has now become a classic study, Francis Madigan (1962) investigated the effects of role satisfaction on length of life.

Over a period of four years (1953-1957), Madigan spent eight months in eight religious houses of an order of Roman Catholic priests in the northeastern United States. Relying on the mortality data meticulously collected by each of the houses, Madigan hypothesized that the priests would have shorter life expectancies than the general population. This hypothesis was derived from two earlier studies in England and Baltimore that showed higher mortality rates among priests, and Madigan's own observations that the priests had high cholesterol diets, tended to be overweight, in poor shape, and heavy smokers. When he compared the death rates of priests to that of married and single white males, his hypothesis was not confirmed. Death rates for priests were consistently and significantly lower at all ages from 15 to 65.

Madigan's post-hoc explanation for the favorable mortality rates of priests stresses the importance of role satisfaction. According to Madigan, ordained priests value their status and role as priests very highly, while seminarians admire their status as candidates for priesthood. Every position in the order carries considerable authority and responsibility. Their self-satisfaction is further enhanced by the prestige given this particular order by both Catholic laity and other orders. On the emotional side, priests usually become members of informal friendship groups, which provide opportunities for relaxation and are a source of emotional support. Finally, "The life of prayer, familiarity with God, and good works which are involved in the role of a religious priest build up a feeling of moral security," which may result in less emotional stress.

Madigan successfully ruled out several alternative explanations for his findings, including the following possibilities:

a   that a selection process screened out unhealthy persons;

b   that the priests experienced less occupational and life stress; and

c   that the priests had lowered metabolism caused by decreased testicular secretions.

However, Rose (1971) suggested that Madigan should have controlled for social class as well. Rose argues that the priests occupy a higher social class and have corresponding higher social-class life styles. Their mortality rates should not have been compared with the general population but with members of the higher social classes. This argument has some merit in that priests are more educated than the general population, but is is debatable if they have a higher social-class life style.

Taken together, the available data convincingly demonstrate that satisfaction with role or occupation and satisfaction with life in general are important contributors to longevity.

CONCLUSION

In this chapter, we have focused on the major biological, social, and psychological determinants of longevity. Little has been said about the relative importance of each, and, unfortunately, the type of research that would answer such questions is still rare. One example is Palmore's (1971a; 1971b) study of volunteers in the Duke Longitudinal Study of Aging. Using multiple regression analysis, he found that *work satisfaction, happiness rating, physical functioning,* and *tobacco use,* in that order, were the four strongest predictors of longevity when age was controlled.

Multivariate analysis techniques are also useful in assessing the relative importance of various predictors of longevity. With this method, it is possible to assess the effects of one variable while holding others constant. Bartko, Patterson, and Butler (1971), for example, used multivariate discriminant analysis and found two variables that were as good discriminators of survivors and nonsurvivors as all of the variables taken together. One was a social psychological variable assessing the degree of organization and complexity of a subject's typical daily behavior and the other was cigarette smoking. The greater the subject's organization of behavior score, the greater was his probability of surviving; smokers had a much higher risk of death. These two variables correctly classified about 80 percent of both survivors and nonsurvivors.

The findings of Palmore (1971a; 1971b) and Bartko et al. (1971) are of limited value for two reasons. First, since neither investigator could include all longevity-relevant variables in their study, the findings are partly determined by the variables the investigators selected. For example, percent overweight may be an important predictor of longevity, but if it isn't included in a particular study, it obviously won't appear in the findings. Second, the findings are based on select and relatively small populations, which limits their generalizability. However, the generalizability of the findings should increase as different experimenters replicate the results with different populations. That cigarette smoking was an important factor in both of the above studies suggests that it is indeed a critical factor affecting longevity.

At present, the most we can say is that the maximum length of the life span is genetically determined, but the many environmental factors such as nutrition, stress, psychological attitudes, social roles, and life styles probably outweigh the genetic factors. As we become more capable of controlling these environmental factors, the genetic factor may become more important.

It is easy to describe the ideal type of longevity research, but for ethical and practical reasons it is sometimes impossible to carry it out. In general, experimental studies with periodic follow-ups would be best. At the minimum, one would need two large groups of persons matched on all variables that might affect longevity. One group would be used as a control and an experimental variable would be deliberately introduced in the other group. If we were interested in the effects of exercise, for example, we might have the experimental group engage in an exercise program. Both experimental and control groups would be studied at regular intervals until all participants in the study died. Such an experiment would be very costly, would take a long time, and would be difficult to implement depending on the variable of interest.

A more reasonable but less rigorous approach is to find two groups of persons who naturally differ on some dimension (e.g., amount of activity or smoking) but who are the same on other relevant dimensions. Again, both groups should be followed for several years, preferably until all members have died. The weakness of this approach is that one can never be sure about how well the two groups are matched. Some unknown selection factor could account for any differences in the longevity of the two groups.

If we can lengthen life, we must then decide what we will do with the extra time. Undoubtedly, a significant increase in longevity would have important economic and social consequences. It is estimated, for example, that a 10-year increase in life span would bankrupt most retirement plans and devastate the already overburdened Social

Security system (Kalish, 1971). It might also change the family structure. Kalish speculates that such an increase

might cause an upsurge in the already increasing divorce rate of those in their fifties and sixties, as well as a comparable increase in marriage and remarriage rates of those in their sixties and seventies.

If another 25 years of healthy and vital life remain after the cementing influence of children is gone, the dissolution of marriage in middle life may become increasingly popular.

Assuming that the economic problems can be solved and that the social problems will solve themselves, the prospect of increased human life-span is very positive. Increasing longevity will probably do more than add years to the period of senility and senescence. As Palmore (1971b) puts it:

It appears probable that the factors associated with longevity are usually associated with such generally desirable qualities as life satisfaction, productivity, and adequate functioning; the expanding longevity research of the future should not only increase the quantity, but should also improve the quality, of human life span.

6

SURVIVING
DEATH:
GRIEF AND
BEREAVEMENT

Death is a group crisis as well as an individual crisis. It involves at least two parties—the person who dies and the survivors who must deal with her or his death. For the individual who dies, death is clearly an ending, but for those who survive, it is a beginning. In many cases, it is a difficult beginning marked by devastating psychological and physical trauma and sometimes even death itself. One of the major goals of this chapter is to examine the impact of death on emotionally involved survivors. Since impact is closely related to the circumstances surrounding a death, two types of bereavement are contrasted: (1) grief caused by a sudden unexpected death, such as an accident, and (2) grief resulting from a predictable death, such as a protracted terminal disease. Since the expression of grief can take many different forms, some of which are maladaptive, the final section of this chapter deals with a variety of therapeutic interventions used to alleviate the stress of bereavement.

BACKGROUND

Grief and bereavement have long been recognized as characteristic human responses to *loss*, whether it be the loss of a person or the loss of some other important organism or object. The research history of bereavement is, however, very short. The pathological potential of grief was recognized by medieval writers, who called grief-induced depression and withdrawal *melancholy*. Grief appears as a specific cause of death in a report published in London in 1657 (Parkes, 1972):

Cause	Number of deaths
Flox and Small Pox	835
Found dead in the streets, etc.	9
French Pox	25
Gout	8
Grief	10
Griping and Plague in the Guts	446
Hang'd and made away 'emselves	24

Two of the early recommended cures for grief-induced melancholia were bleeding and liberal doses of opium, practices which persisted well into the nineteenth century.

Freud is often credited as one of the first to develop a systematic explanation of the psychodynamics of grief. In 1915, Freud argued that grief represents a breakdown of the denial of death. That is, the mourner grieves because he or she can no longer deny the reality of death (Glick, Weiss, and Parkes, 1974). This view was revised two years later and appeared in *Mourning and Melancholia*. Briefly, Freud believed that grief is a process by which the individual progressively withdraws the energy that ties him or her to the object of his or her love (Glick et al., 1974):

This energy was conceived by Freud as being bound to the memories and ideas that arose from interaction with the dead person. To become free of his tie to this person, the energy has to be detached by a process that Freud termed "hypercathexis," a process that requires the mourner to turn his back on the real world, and to invest free energy in the struggle to "decathect" the loved object. By focusing his mind on the lost person and bringing to consciousness each relevant memory, the mourner gradually sets free the bound up energy.

This view of bereavement is consistent with observations that newly bereaved people often obsess over memories of the dead person and spend a great deal of time mentally reliving the events leading up to the death. Freud's theory also suggests a more positive outcome for the bereaved person who faces up to the loss than for one who avoids thinking about it. We shall see later that this observation is roughly consistent with the data.

An alternative theory of grief was developed by John Bowlby, an English psychoanalyst (Glick et al., 1974). According to Bowlby, each person has a few significant others to whom she or he is very attached and to whom she or he wishes to remain physically and psychologically close. Separation from these individuals evokes behavior patterns that attempt to restore closeness, and the strength of these behaviors vary as a function of the length of the separation and the presence or absence of danger for either party. That is, the longer the separation and the greater the danger, the stronger the behaviors. These behaviors are gradually extinguished as the individual realizes that the longed-for reunion will not occur. It should be noted that this view differs significantly from Freud's view that grieving behavior serves the function of detaching the individual from the one who has gone. In situations where the loss is permanent, Bowlby stresses that grieving behaviors are maladaptive because they try to accomplish something that is impossible under the circumstances.

Yet another view of grief is advocated by C. Murray Parkes (Parkes, 1972). He describes grief as a process of realization whereby internal awareness is brought in line with external events. The modification of a person's internal world takes time and is aided by the repeated discrepancies encountered when remembering the deceased in an environment where the deceased no longer exists. The awareness of this discrepancy between the outside world and internal awareness leads to frustration. Since being continually frustrated is an aversive state, the behaviors (such as dwelling on the loss) producing frustration are eventually extinguished and the grieving process comes gradually to an end.

None of the three theoretical perspectives are stated explicitly enough to allow rigorous testing of their validity. Each is vague enough to make falsification by conventional scientific means impossible. In Freud's model, for example, the ambiguity of the term "energy" makes it difficult to test the validity of his theory. *Mental energy* is somehow analogous to physical energy in Freud's theory, but it is difficult to imagine how one might measure level of mental energy. The theories may be best viewed as rough guides to understanding the process and meaning of bereavement.

Examples of more descriptive approaches to the study of bereavement are plentiful. More than 40 years ago, an entire issue of the *Journal of Abnormal and Social Psychology* (1933) was devoted to articles on bereavement. In that issue, Thomas Eliot wrote an article entitled "A step toward the social psychology of bereavement," in which he called for the application of the "modern techniques of case histories, group studies, and documentary analysis" to the study of death in general and bereavement in particular. Eliot presented a detailed outline for the analysis of narratives and case studies of bereavement.

In the same issue, another psychologist, Howard Becker (1933), discussed differences in the manifestations of the primary emotion, sorrow. Relying on the writings of A. E. Shand (1920), personal observations, and examples taken from literature, Becker described manifestations of sorrow ranging from violent outward expression,

> *She willfully her sorrow did augment*
> *And offered hope of comfort did despise;*
> *Her golden locks most cruelly she rent*
> *And scratched her face with ghastly detriment.*
> (*from Spenser,* Faerie Queene)

to a calm stoicism where the sufferer remains outwardly mute,

The sentiment which attends the sudden revelation that all is lost, silently is gathered up into the heart; it is too deep for gestures or for words; and no part of it passes to the outside.
> (*from deQuincey,* Suspiria de Profundis)

Becker reviewed Shand's "laws of sorrow" and criticized his heavy reliance on instinct and introspection. It would be too time consuming to discuss all of Shand's 23 *laws of sorrow*. Several have been verified by subsequent research and inspection. Law 10, for example, states,

In proportion as the event which causes sorrow is both sudden and unexpected, it tends to arouse surprise, and therefore to increase the intensity of sorrow.

This law is complemented by Law 11,

In proportion as the event which causes sorrow either occurs gradually or is foreseen, the sorrow on that account tends to be felt with less intensity or strength.

ANTICIPATED AND UNANTICIPATED DEATH

Taken together, Laws 10 and 11 make a distinction that was noted in the literature almost four decades later. Robert Fulton (1970) differentiates a *high grief death*, one which is accidental, sudden, or involves a young person, from a *low grief death*, involving a prolonged illness or an old person. He argues that there is less grief in the latter case because the bereaved goes through a period of anticipating grief before the death occurs. Glick et al. disagree with this view, arguing that the predeath response should not be characterized as a grieving process. According to them, the person experiencing an anticipated loss does not reorganize himself or herself cognitively and emotionally so that he or she has grieved before the death occurs. If this were true, we would expect anticipated and unanticipated grief to follow the same course, with anticipated grief having an earlier onset. This is not the case, however.

Unanticipated bereavement is different both quantitatively and qualitatively from grief resulting from a predictable death. The consequences of an anticipated loss are generally less severe for both men and women. Weiss et al. report data showing that the probability of remarriage and adaptive reorganization is greater among widows whose husbands died predictably as a result of a protracted illness than it is for widows whose husbands died unexpectedly. The findings for widowers were similar though less strong.

What might account for these differences in outcomes for the anticipated and unanticipated deaths? Fulton identifies four stages in the process of anticipating grief:

1   depression
2   heightened concern for the ill person
3   rehearsal of the death
4   an attempt to adjust to the consequences of the death

The first stage, *depression*, is undoubtedly an accurate description of the initial response to an impending death, but it is unlikely that feeling depressed prior to death lessens the negative emotional response after the death. In fact, the reverse may be true. Bornstein, Clayton, Halikas, Maurice, and Robin (1973) found that feelings of depression before death were not associated with decreased grief afterward. Interview data collected from widows of all ages in Cincinnati revealed that those who reported being depressed prior to the death were more likely to be depressed afterwards. Similarly, Glick et al. (1974), in their study of Cambridge widows, found that those who were most upset by their husband's illness were likely to be most upset by his death. The evidence suggests then, that predeath depression does not diminish post-death emotional trauma.

Fulton's second stage, *heightened concern for the ill person*, is probably a better candidate for explaining the differences in anticipated and non-anticipated bereavement. To the extent that guilt contributes to traumatic bereavement responses, persons who had the opportunity to suffer with and for the deceased should feel less guilty and should, therefore, evidence fewer negative bereavement effects. Obviously, the wife who anticipates her husband's death has a much greater opportunity to expiate herself than the wife who suddenly finds her husband dead and subsequently dwells on all the things she could have done for her husband but didn't.

Fulton's third and fourth stages, *rehearsal of the death* and an *attempt to adjust to the consequences of the death*, are also critical in explaining the differences in impact between anticipated and non-anticipated deaths. Two decades of experimental, social-psychology research have taught us that stressful life events are less aversive to the extent that they are predictable. This is partly due to the fact that organisms can brace themselves for predictable stressors; they can muster the appropriate coping mechanisms and thereby diminish the impact of the stressor. The opportunity to rehearse and prepare for a death is undoubtedly very important in minimizing the effects of the loss. Making attempts to adjust to the consequences of a death serves a similar function. By thinking through and preparing for the anticipated death, the post-death period becomes more controllable for the bereaved individual. Being prepared should make the bereaved feel less helpless and give them feelings of greater control of their lives.

A final important consequence of an anticipated death is that death is perceived as less mysterious and hence less frightening. An anticipated death may be traumatic when it finally occurs, but its cause is understood. A specific disease with a predictable course is usually involved. As a result, the widow or widower knows what to fear and can, to some extent, plan her or his life to avoid or minimize the possibility of encountering the same disease again.

When death occurs suddenly and unexpectedly, as in an accident, suicide, or murder, the survivors never really understand why the death occurred. Survivors often live with the fear that the event could occur again either to someone else close or to the bereaved survivors themselves. For example, it is not uncommon to find a widow afraid to go out in the evening because her husband was shot at night; or a widower who enters an automobile with trepidation because his wife was killed in an auto accident, or finally, one whose husband or wife has died in a fire and who forever after is uneasy in the house at night. For these individuals, death is a constant presence that could strike again as unpredictably as before.

For many, the fear of another unexpected death is great enough to preclude remarriage. Glick et al. (1974) observed that

the one critical difference among widows was that those who did not anticipate their husband's death did not move toward remarriage. Indeed, they rejected the idea of remarriage even when pressed to remarry by a boyfriend, by their children, or by their immediate kin, even in two cases when they had a child with the boyfriend. Why should this have been so? A frequent comment . . . was that they did not want again to risk unanticipated loss or to place their children in a situation where they too must risk another such loss. . . . They have become phobic toward marriage.

SYMPTOMATOLOGY OF GRIEF

In what is now considered a classic paper on grief, Eric Lindemann (1944) differentiated normal from morbid grief precipitated by *high grief deaths*. His aim was to sensitize medical practitioners to specific symptoms of grief and to suggest appropriate treatment procedures. Lindemann's observations were based on a study of 101 patients, including neurotic patients who died in the hospital, bereaved disaster victims of the Cocoanut Grove fire in Boston and their close relatives, and relatives of members of the armed forces.

Lindemann observed the following symptoms common to all individuals suffering from acute grief:

1   somatic distress occurring repeatedly and lasting from 20 minutes to an hour at a time
2   a feeling of tightness in the throat
3   choking with shortness of breath

4   a need for sighing

5   an empty feeling in the abdomen

6   loss of muscular power

7   an intense subjective distress described as tension or mental pain

Psychologically, these individuals were preoccupied with an image of the deceased and feelings of guilt. Behaviorally, the bereaved often became hostile toward friends and relatives, showed frenzied activity with an inability to complete tasks, were very restless, unable to sit still, moved about in aimless fashion, and continually searched for something to do. At the same time, they lacked the ability to maintain organized patterns of activity.

The duration of grief depended largely on how well the individual carried out his *grief work*. Patients had to recognize and accept the discomfort of bereavement before an adjustment to the environment in which the deceased was missing was possible. Lindemann observed that, for a long time, male survivors of the Cocoanut Grove fire appeared to be in a state of tension, with tightened facial musculature, and unable to relax for fear that they might break down. Once they were willing to accept the grief, the recovery process began. Under psychiatric care, most of the individuals exhibiting normal grief reactions recovered in four to six weeks.

NORMAL GRIEF

Lindemann's capsule summary of a normal grief response is substantially supported by the findings of subsequent researchers such as Parkes (1972) and Glick et al. (1974). Furthermore, the latter researchers have fleshed out Lindemann's outline and have provided important descriptive details of the typical grieving process.

The normal grief response can roughly be divided into three phases, each with its own temporal boundaries and characteristic behavioral responses.

Initial response
The first phase starts when the death occurs and continues for a few weeks after the funeral. The bereaved reacts to the death with shock and disbelief. She or he reports feeling cold, numb, dazed, empty, and

confused. The numbness and disbelief serve as a barrier against the overwhelming pain and sorrow that the bereaved perceive as unbearable. This initial reaction lasts for several days and then gives way to an all-encompassing sorrow, expressed through extended periods (sometimes several weeks long) of crying and weeping.

During this period, the bereaved are often in conflict over whether to respond to their own gut feelings or to the implicit, and sometimes explicit, desires of those who would like them to be composed and in control. Consider the case of Mrs. M., who was discouraged from displaying emotion by her husband before his death (Glick et al., 1974):

Last year he said to me, "If anything ever happens to me I don't want you to go to pieces. I want you to act like Jacqueline Kennedy—you know, very brave and courageous. You've got to have class," he said. "I just don't want you screaming and hollering."

So I just prayed to God to give me the courage to do that, and He did. I didn't even cry at the funeral, and it was an impressive funeral. But I did what he asked me to do. I behaved as he wanted me to.

I was worried how I was going to react at the funeral home: "Gee, I hope I don't—I hope I'm alright." Then when it was the day of the funeral, "Gee, I hope I'm alright." I didn't know how I would react. But I acted very good. I just cried quiet, I prayed, I said my final prayers, and I touched his arm, that's all. I just kept thinking about him telling me not to cry. Now I don't break down very often—once in a while when I'm alone I will—but during the Mass I didn't shed one tear. And at the cemetery I didn't shed one tear.

As time passes, physicians, relatives and friends are likely to equate controlling one's emotions with "doing well." As the pressures to behave normally increase, the bereaved person is encouraged to inhibit emotional responses. The long-term consequences of these demands are probably positive. As long as the bereaved does not perceive the demands as unreasonable, he or she is likely to respond by inhibiting grief behaviors and suffer no additional negative consequences. Social psychologists such as Daryl Bem (1967) have argued that people do not decide how they feel and then behave accordingly;

instead, they observe their own behaviors and then decide how they feel. If this is true, and evidence suggests that it is, bereaved persons should feel better after observing that their rate of weeping and crying has decreased.

In addition to sorrow, the bereaved must next learn to deal with runaway anxiety and the fear of a breakdown. Many of the widows in the Glick et al. (1974) study expressed fears of not making it, losing their minds, breaking down, etc. Mrs. F's statement, made three weeks after her husband's death, reveals these fears:

Some days I'm worried about having a nervous breakdown. Sometimes I get more nervous than others, and I just feel like I'm ready to scream, especially if I'm alone. Like sometimes at night I'm sitting here and I just feel like I'm ready to scream. I'll put the music on to listen to that, or I'll sing to the records, just something to do, so that you re not talking to yourself. I think it helps. It helps me. I don't know if it would anybody else, but I'll just put the records on and I'll sing along with the records. Some people think I'm soft, but it really helps me.

In almost all cases, individuals who were overwhelmed by this free-floating anxiety recognized the potential danger of this state and developed coping mechanisms to deal with it. Some turned to tranquilizers, sleeping pills, or alcohol, while others tried to keep themselves busy to suppress the fears and anxieties. Glick et al. reported that 28 percent of the widows studied increased their intake of alcohol and 27 percent took tranquilizers. These rates of use were significantly higher than for a matched group of nonbereaved controls. Among widowers, the largest increase was found in alcohol use. Men did not significantly increase their use of tranquilizers.

Lindemann (1944) described the psycho-physiological symptoms accompanying bereavement as an empty feeling in the abdomen, shortness of breath, tightness in the throat, and loss of muscular power. Other commonly reported symptoms included sleeplessness, loss of appetite, irritability, muscular aches and pains, lethargy, headaches, menstrual irregularities and, in some cases, the bereaved exhibited some of the symptoms of the illness that caused the death. These symptoms are typically not incapacitating and are not as threatening as the psychological distress. After the first three weeks of bereavement, the frequency of these symptoms decreased and appeared only briefly for the remainder of the first year of bereavement.

Intermediate phase

The second phase of normal bereavement begins several weeks after the leave-taking ceremonies, when the widow or widower must confront the reality of daily living without the lost spouse. This phase begins roughly three weeks after the death and terminates approximately a year later. Three distinct behavior patterns characterize this phase. First, the mourner engages in obsessional review; the bereaved uncontrollably dwells on one or several scenes associated with the death. The mourner might berate herself or himself with thoughts like, "If I had only made him wear his seat belt" or "If I had only forced her to go to the doctor sooner." In this manner, important choice points leading to the death are reviewed, alternative paths imagined, and different outcomes generated. With time, the futility of these reviews is recognized and the real outcome—death—is accepted.

The second aspect is a search for meaning for the death. The bereaved wants to understand why it happened and asks, "Why did this have to happen?" Mrs. E's statement is typical (Glick et al., 1974):

I wish somebody could just sit down and explain to me why a young man had to die. A lot of people have died, but I still want to know why it had to happen to him. With the children, you say, "God does things." But I still can't understand why he had to die. I know it's God's way, because he wouldn't have died if God hadn't intended it for him, he'd have went through all that and walked out with a little scratch if it hadn't been time for him to go.

The same feelings are expressed by Mrs. L.:

I've asked myself why but I have no answer. Why, why, why, why was it him? What did he do? But I just have no answer. I don't know, I ask myself every day.

For some, the answer is simply that it was God's will, for others a completely satisfying answer is never found.

Perhaps the most intriguing aspect of the second phase is a process best described as searching for the deceased. Many of the activities that were previously shared tend to psychologically evoke the presence of the deceased. Watching TV in the evening, for example, may cause the bereaved to feel that the dead spouse is present and sharing the experience with them. In some cases, the sense of presence is so strong that widows actually have illusions of having seen or heard their dead husbands (Parkes, 1972). A perceptual set is developed, designed to detect the presence of the spouse. The bereaved may further find themselves moving toward likely locations where the deceased might be encountered. Finally, the bereaved may actually call out for the lost spouse and expect a response. This phenomenon is most frequent among individuals whose spouse died suddenly and unexpectedly.

More than any other aspect of human grieving, the searching for the deceased is most analogous to animal bereavement. Lorenz describes the response of the greylag goose that has been separated from its mate (Parkes, 1972):

The first response to the disappearance of the partner consists in the anxious attempt to find him again. The goose moves about restlessly by day and night, flying great distances and visiting places where the partner might be found, uttering all the time the penetrating trisyllabic long-distance call. . . The searching expeditions are extended farther and farther, and quite often the searcher himself gets lost, or succumbs to an accident. . . All the objectively observable characteristics of the goose's behavior on losing its mate are roughly identical with. . .human grief. . .

Similarly, Bowlby (1961) summarizes the bereavement responses of the jackdaw, goose, domestic dog, orangutan, and chimpanzee as follows:

Members of lower species protest at the loss of a loved object and do all in their power to seek and recover it; hostility, externally directed, is frequent; withdrawal, rejection of a potential new object, apathy, and restlessness are the rule.

The frequency of all three types of phase-two behavior—obsessional review, the search for an understanding of the death, and the search for the presence of the deceased—decreases with time. For most persons, functional stability returns within a few months after the death and for many full recovery is achieved by the end of a year. Glick et al. (1974) report that 61 percent of the widows studied agreed with the statement, "I'm beginning to feel more like myself again" several months after the death. By the end of the year, most widows felt that they had "done well," "were more in control of their lives and themselves," and "were less likely to give way to tears" (Glick et al., 1974). Only a few widows had recovered very little, were still despairing the loss of their husband, and continued to have chaotic lives. Twenty-eight percent of the widows agreed, at the end of the first year, with the statement, "I would not care if I died tomorrow."

Recovery phase

With the beginning of the second year after the death, survivors embark on the third and last phase of bereavement, the *recovery phase*. It is often preceded by a conscious decision by the bereaved that dwelling on the past is fruitless and that life must now proceed. The forward motion takes several forms. Most bereaved persons become more aggressive socially; the previous reluctance to enter into social situations diminishes and the bereaved may, for the first time, actually seek out social encounters. For some, the attempt at social participation is initially an aversive experience because they find themselves assigned to peripheral status. They are treated as stigmatized persons, not unlike the handicapped (Glick et al., 1974):

Being a widow is just something extraordinary. You don't belong. You're a widow, you know, as if you were a freak or something. I wear my wedding ring all the time. I don't tell people I'm a widow. Strangers, they say, "You're married?" And I say, "Sure." It's easier. You feel better that way.

Like a phoenix rising out of the ashes, a widow or widower often comes out of the bereavement experience a more capable and stronger person. One reason for this is that he or she can take pride in having dealt with and survived a devastating event. Many widows look back a year after the death and view their recovery as a little short of miraculous. Most thought that they could never do it and are amazed that they did, in fact, pull through. Who gets the credit for their survival? An answer is provided by the widow who says, "I fought my way back, so maybe I'm stronger than I ever realized." Thus many bereaved come to perceive themselves as possessing great strength for dealing with emotional crisis.

A second source of self-confidence is a large repertoire of daily living skills that had to be acquired in order to survive. Almost all the widows in the Glick et al. study developed new skills that they had considered beyond their capacities before their husbands died, such as minor house repairs, lawn and car care, balancing check books, driving a car—all these are skills that had to be acquired in order to survive. For many, the acquisition of necessary survival skills was only a beginning. The sense of competence from mastering these skills let them venture into activities they had previously deemed inappropriate or too difficult (e.g., ice skating, attending school, traveling). If there is anything positive about surviving the death of someone close to us it is the possibility of increased growth and self-confidence, although this self-improvement comes at a very high price.

MORBID GRIEF REACTIONS

Atypical or morbid grief reactions are not qualitatively different from normal grief responses; they differ only in intensity and duration. For example, statements like, "I miss him every moment of the day; I want my husband every minute of the day but neither you nor anybody else can give him to me" (Parkes, 1972) would be considered normal bereavement responses if made a few weeks after the death. If they were made one-and-a-half or nine years after the death, they would be identified as morbid or abnormal grief responses.

In his study of bereavement, Lindemann (1944) observed that the most striking feature of the morbid grief reaction is the delay in emotional response for several weeks or longer. During this interim, the bereaved individual exhibits a sense of well-being and zeal. But as a result of this internalization of the grief response, these individuals are susceptible to psychosomatic disorders which cause permanent physiological harm. Lindemann reported that 31 of 41 morbid-grief patients developed ulcerative colitis shortly after the loss of an important person. Other diseases were rheumatoid arthritis and asthma. The period of apparent calm is usually followed by a gross change in behavior, including intense hostility directed at specific individuals, irritability towards friends and relatives, and inability to initiate any activity unless primed by someone else.

In addition, patients behave in ways detrimental to their social and economic well-being. Some individuals in Lindemann's study, for instance, gave away all their possessions, engaged in foolish economic dealings, or lost their friends and professional standing by a series of "stupid acts." The grief reaction was finally found to lead to a state of "agitated depression with tension, agitation, insomnia, feelings of worthlessness, bitter self-accusation, and obvious need for punishments."

Descriptive information about morbid grief reactions comes to us primarily from bereaved persons who sought professional help for problems associated with the death. Parkes (1972) reports the results of an investigation of 35 bereaved males and females who sought and obtained professional help. The majority (26 of 35) of these persons sought help for depression; six had problems with alcoholism; five had hypochondriacal symptoms; and four had phobic symptoms. In addition, smaller numbers had problems with panic attacks, asthma, loss of hair, depersonalization, insomnia, fainting, and headaches. Two persons exhibited psychoses with hallucinations and delusions. These symptoms are not peculiar to morbid grief reactions.

Of the symptoms listed, guilt or self-reproach and symptom identification with the deceased typically vary in both intensity and frequency. Two-thirds of Parkes's (1972) bereaved psychiatric patients expressed intense guilt and self-blame in relation to the deceased. Their self-reproach varied from mild blame, because the widow felt that she could have done more for her dying husband, to severe self-criticism because the widow felt directly responsible for her husband's death.

Instances of symptom identification were also more frequent among the psychiatric patients. Several widows developed aches and pains in the same site as their dead husband. Several patients experienced pain in the chest, resembling the pain of coronary thrombosis, and another had pain simulating lung cancer. One women, whose husband was left unable to speak by a stroke, became speechless for ten days after his death. Parkes (1972) further reports an interesting case of symptom identification with a relative other than the deceased.

A woman who showed little grief shortly after her sister's death became paralyzed and anesthetic from the waist down seven months later.

These symptoms were identical to her mother's who, many years earlier, developed paralysis of the legs after the death of the patient's two brothers.

Such *identification phenomenon* were consistently more common among those with morbid grief than those with normal grief.

By definition, the long-term prognosis for morbid grief reactions is not very favorable. The incidence of physical disease, prolonged emotional trauma, and grief-related death is significantly higher for persons who fall into this category.

PHYSIOLOGICAL AND BEHAVIORAL CONSEQUENCES OF GRIEF

We have described the temporal and emotional course of both typical and atypical grief. It is clear from these descriptions that the process of bereavement is by no means a pleasant experience, although good may come of it. When individual cases are examined, the data clearly show that bereavement can result in devastating physiological and behavioral changes. We have not yet answered the question, "Do the bereaved in general suffer significantly more negative physiological and behavioral effects than the nonbereaved?" With few exceptions, the answer to this question is a strong yes.

Studies linking bereavement with one or more negative behavioral or physiological outcomes are numerous. Parents who lose a child, for instance, often exhibit behavioral changes that adversely affect their surviving offspring (Binger, Feurstein, Kushner, Zoger, and Mikkelson, 1959; Natterson and Knudson, 1960; Bozeman, Orbach, and Sutherland, 1955; Friedman and Zaris, 1963; Hamovitch, 1964). Children who lose their parents or sibling typically have more problems in later life than nonbereaved children (Markusen and Fulton, 1971; Gauthier, 1966; Granville-Grossman, 1966). Markusen and Fulton, for example, presented statistical evidence showing that persons who lost a parent during childhood married and divorced more often and had higher crime rates. Although the literature on childhood bereavement is quite extensive, it is difficult to draw conclusions on the effects of bereavement alone because of the long time lag between the death of a parent and the appearance of a behavioral disturbance. By far, the most convincing evidence demonstrating the negative effects of bereavement *per se* comes from studies of widows and widowers.

Newsweek (1967) called it the *Broken Heart Syndrome*. Relying on data collected by Rees and Lutkins, *Newsweek* reported that a death in the family greatly increases the mortality rates among close relatives, especially the surviving spouse. Rees and Lutkins studied records of the relatives of 371 residents of Llanidloes, Wales, who died over a six-year period. Mortality rates among relatives were compared with a matched control group from the same community. Within the first year of bereavement, the mortality rate among relatives was seven times higher than among the controls (4.76 percent vs. 0.68 percent). This difference was most striking when the bereaved and controls were compared (12.2 percent vs. 1.2 percent). The suddenness of death also proved to be a factor. The risk of a bereaved relative dying within one year was more than twice as high if the relative died suddenly in a hospital rather than slowly at home. The ages of the deceased and the survivor also attenuates the effect of bereavement. A study on long-term adaptation to bereavement in the elderly by Heyman and Gianturco (1973) revealed no long-term physical deterioration effects of bereavement.

These findings have been replicated in both England and the United States by numerous investigators (Cox and Ford, 1970; Young, Bernard, and Wallis, 1970; Mathison, 1970; Hyman, 1969; Parkes, 1964; Kraus and Lilienfeld, 1959; Kutscher, Schoenberg, and Carr, 1970; and Schoenberg, 1969). These data consistently show that the risk of dying is at least twice as great for widows and widowers for a great variety of diseases. Although this relationship is easy to find, explaining it and ruling out alternative explanations is more difficult. Although no single investigation has been able to rule out all alternative hypotheses, it is possible to view the studies collectively and assess the validity of the various explanations for the high mortality rates of widows and widowers. Each of these possible explanations will be considered in some detail below.

The selection hypothesis

This explanation contends that the mortality rates reported in most studies are artifactual because the widowed who are in good health tend to remarry quickly and return themselves to the married population, while the ill who become widowed tend to remain widowed and are classified as such on their death certificates when they die. Thus those not remarrying would appear to have the higher mortality rates because the healthier widowed persons remarried.

Evidence contradicting this explanation was reported by Young, Bernard, and Wallis (1970), Cox and Ford (1970), and Kraus and Lilienfeld (1959). Young, Bernard, and Wallis found in a study of 4486 widowers that the deleterious impact of being widowed was greatest during the first six months of widowhood. Cox and Ford replicated this finding and, in addition, pointed out that after two years of widowhood mortality rates among the widowed decline to a level equal to that of married persons. Kraus and Lilienfeld reported that, on the average, those widowed individuals who remarry do so more than two years after being widowed. For the selection hypothesis to be correct, these individuals would have had to remarry within six months after becoming widowed.

The mutual choice of poor-risk mates or homogamy hypothesis

Both Young, Bernard, and Wallis (1970) and Kraus and Lilienfeld (1959) reported that there is a tendency for the unfit to marry the unfit and the fit to marry the fit. Individuals with apparent disabilities of the limbs or sense organs tend to marry persons with comparable disabilities. One might further argue that if psychological character- istics are important in the etiology of some diseases, then mates choosing each other on similar traits should die at about the same time and of the same disease. Unfortunately, there exists only one study (Ciocco, 1940) showing a tendency for husbands and wives to die of the same disease. Of 2571 husbands and wives studied during a period from 1898 to 1938, there was a nonsignificant tendency for husbands and wives to die from the same cause when either tuberculosis, influenza, pneumonia, heart disease, or cancer was the cause of death. The strongest relationships involved the first two causes, but this is probably best explained by the presence of a common infectious environment.

The common unfavorable environment hypothesis

This explanation simply argues that two people living together are exposed to the same environmental risks. They eat the same kinds of food, expose themselves to similar dangers, and, therefore, die at approximately the same time. Although it probably accounts for some of the early deaths among the bereaved, it cannot account for all of them. For example, this explanation cannot account for the greater impact of a sudden death as compared to a slow, lingering death. Like the previous explanation, this one predicts that couples die of the same disease, but this is a relatively rare occurrence. This type of explanation also cannot account for increased psychological problems among widows whose husbands died of direct physical causes.

The desolation effect hypothesis

Invariably, researchers come to believe that the negative effects of widowhood are mostly due to something they refer to as loss of will to live, hopelessness, the giving up complex, or the broken heart syndrome. The state of hopelessness, it is argued, results in direct physiological changes such as lowered resistance to diseases and/or in behavioral changes detrimental to the individual's well-being. A number of physiological changes induced by stress are discussed in detail in the chapter on longevity; it will be useful now to examine some physiological reactions induced by the stress of bereavement.

Jerome Fredrick (1971), relying primarily on literature on the effects of prolonged stress on animals, depicted a causal chain that may account for the high mortality rates of the bereaved in all categories of disease. The physiological process he proposed begins with the overstimulation of the pituitary, which results in the production of excess quantities of adrenocorticotropic hormones (ACTH). This, in turn, causes the adrenal cortex to increase the level of corticosteroids. One of the physiological consequences of increased levels of corticosteroids is the suppression of the inflammatory response, which is essential for adequate functioning of the immunity mechanism. With the suppression of the immunity mechanism, the bereaved person becomes more susceptible to bacterial, fungal, and viral infection. The possible lowered resistance to disease may be additionally precipitated by physically detrimental behavior. The bereaved may not get enough rest, may neglect taking medication, or may even ignore serious medical problems. Parkes (1964) found that widows had inadequate rest and did not eat enough due to loss of appetite. However, Parkes also found that the widows did not neglect seeking treatment for their illnesses.

The nongrief-related behavior changes hypothesis
The death of a spouse may also result in neglect and high-risk behavior that is not directly related to bereavement. Perhaps the surviving mate doesn't eat properly, take medicine, or go to the doctor when ill, not because she or he is grief-stricken, but simply because the deceased spouse isn't there to encourage (nag) her or him to do all these things. The likelihood of having an auto accident may be higher, for instance, due to the absence of a spouse who typically helped the other watch the road.

Conclusion
Five possible explanations that might account for the high mortality rates of the bereaved have been discussed. Only three of the five—common unfavorable environment, desolation, and nongrief-related behavior changes—were not ruled out when the relevant evidence was examined. The desolation hypothesis is cited most often and probably accounts for most of the negative effects of bereavement. A recent cross-cultural study on bereavement further illustrates the validity of the desolation hypothesis. Yamamoto (1970) compared mortality rates among widows in London, Boston, and Tokyo and found the characteristically high death rates among widows in all groups except the highly religious Japanese. Yamamoto attributed the low rates among the Japanese widows to their commitment to Buddhism which stresses ancestor worship. Presumably, the Japanese widows are able to sense the presence of their husbands even after the death. This makes it less necessary for them to grieve.

While the several alternative hypotheses have been ruled out, the remaining explanation is in need of further refinement before the process of bereavement is adequately understood for effective treatment. A recent study by Morgan (1976) represents a step in this direction. Morgan investigated morale and life satisfaction among 232 widowed and 363 married women from 45 to 74 years of age. Instead of simply looking for differences in life satisfaction and morale between widowed and nonwidowed women, she examined the effects of several mediating variables that might account for observed differences on these dimensions. Controlling for income and employment status, she found that the difference in morale between the two groups disappeared. That is, individuals equated for income and employment status did not differ in morale, regardless of marital status. This suggests that it is the loss of support that accounts for the low morale of the bereaved.

Clayton (1973) provides a case study that illustrates this point.

A taxi driver with no living relatives was admitted to the hospital and diagnosed as having alcoholic Korsacoff's syndrome. Before her death, his wife had ridden with him in the taxi, giving him street directions and company. His wife's death deprived him of both companionship and income. The loss of his wife may have been psychologically devastating but it also clearly affected his economic status.

Further research is needed to untangle the effects of the many contributing factors associated with bereavement.

HELPING THE BEREAVED

Geoffrey Gorer (1965) describes successful grief work as consisting of three stages:

1   The bereaved must separate himself or herself from the deceased by breaking the bond that holds them together.

2   He must readjust to an environment from which the deceased is missing.

3   He must form new relationships.

Few psychologists or psychiatrists would disagree with these goals (see Bowlby, 1960; Lindemann, 1944; and Golan, 1975), but many would argue over how they are best achieved. In the remaining section of this chapter, we examine the available intervention strategies and their effectiveness in making grief work a success.

In most cases, grief resolves itself over time. Within three to four years after death, most widows are happily engaged in life and perceive their lives to be at least as rich and fulfilling as they were before the death. Many, in fact, perceive themselves as stronger and more capable for having succeeded in overcoming their loss. Only a minority of bereaved individuals, approximately 25 percent, require any kind of professional or paraprofessional help.

Are there any general rules for treating the bereaved? Glick et al. (1974) advocate anything that promotes feelings of security and safety and the elimination of all possible dangers and uncertainties. Providing the bereaved individual with familiar surroundings, people, and situations maximizes feelings of security. Although a brief change of scenery may provide some psychological distance from the deceased, the newly bereaved should be discouraged from moving out of a previously shared apartment or house. Moreover, the bereaved should be surrounded by familiar people such as family members and friends. Professional support such as the clergy may also be beneficial. The bereaved should be encouraged to continue in familiar roles, and to accept new ones, but shouldn't be pushed into roles that are too taxing or beyond the person's capabilities. A failure experience at this time would only reinforce feelings of helplessness. Finally, feelings of safety are enhanced by making an escape route available. An escape route might be a neighbor who says, "Drop by when things get tough," a job, or a tranquilizer or sedative—anything that gives the bereaved the feeling that there are crutches available to help them regain control.

Professional therapy

When an individual exhibits a morbid grief reaction, professional or paraprofessional intervention is called for. A variety of therapeutic strategies have been advocated for the treatment of the bereaved. Lindemann (1944) for example, advocates transforming a morbid grief reaction into normal grief and then resolving the normal grief. Lindemann provides a very detailed description of a morbid grief response, but gives few specific suggestions for accomplishing the transformation into normal grief. The psychiatrist's most important task, he argues, is to share the patient's grief work and help the patient extricate herself or himself from the bondage of the deceased and find new, rewarding interaction patterns. This is generally achieved by encouraging the patient to express the pain of bereavement by verbalizing the sorrow, sense of loss, and feelings of guilt. Special techniques are called for if the grief reaction is marked by hostility or if intense depression is the primary feature. The hostile and angry person should be encouraged to express his or her hostility toward the psychiatrist without inducing guilt feelings that might cause him or her to avoid future interviews with the therapist. Intense depression can be treated with antidepressant drugs such as imipramine or phenelzine.

Once the pain of bereavement has been accepted and special problems have been dealt with, the therapist can proceed with methods used for the treatment of normal grief reactions. The patient should be encouraged to review her or his relationship with the deceased and formulate a new relationship with the deceased as a dead person. And, finally, the patient should be encouraged to acquire new behavior patterns with surviving friends and relatives. All this can be accomplished in eight to ten interviews with the therapist.

Psychiatrist Vamik Volkan (in Horn, 1974) and his colleagues have developed a *regriefing therapy* for individuals exhibiting pathological mourning. The technique overlaps with Lindemann's, stressing the importance of getting the patient to exhibit an emotional response to the loss. This is accomplished by taking the patient through the original grief process a second time with the aim of getting him or her to accept the death emotionally as well as intellectually. The dammed-up emotions can often be released by discovering the patient's particular "linking object"—some memento such as a photograph, jewelry, or a letter, which connects the bereaved with the deceased—and confronting her or him with it. Over time, the linking objects should be replaced with what Glick et al. (1974) call connecting or *bridging objects* or behavior such as a new car, learning how to drive, going back to school, making new friends, etc. Symbolically, these phenomena represent a commitment to a new life, one that is future-oriented rather than focused on the past.

Paraprofessional therapy

Numerous national and local organizations have been created to aid the bereaved in their adjustment to a new environment. At a workshop for widows and widowers held at the Harvard Medical School, for example, representatives from organizations like Parents without Partners, Carmel Club, Escathon Club, Catholic Widow and Widowers Club, and Women's Fellowship Group gave their views on how best to help the bereaved family. The common feature of all these clubs is that members have lost a husband or a wife and have therefore gone through the bereavement process themselves. They assume that someone who has experienced bereavement can best help the recently bereaved, and according to their own reports they have been very successful.

One "experimental" preventive intervention program has been much publicized, the Widow to Widow Program by Phyllis Silverman of Harvard Medical School (1969). It is fashioned after existing widow and widower clubs in that widows are used to contact the recently bereaved to help them with emotional and practical problems. Although Silverman calls the program an experiment in preventive intervention, she has not run the appropriate control groups that would enable her to adequately document the effectiveness of the program. The available data, however, suggest that the program is a useful one. In one study (Silverman and Cooperband, 1975), 50 of 99 widows contacted were receptive to being contacted by another widow. Those that did not accept the visiting widow's offer for help either did not need help or were receiving sufficient help from friends and relatives. Follow-up interviews carried out three years after the women became widowed showed that those who refused help had assessed their situation accurately. There was no evidence of long-term deleterious effects among this group of natural copers. Results for those that did accept the offer were similarly positive, although these conclusions are based on the impressions of the visiting widows.

What makes the widow-to-widow program work? Three factors seem important. First, the visiting widows provide a sympathetic ear for the bereaved. Their sympathy is likely to be perceived as sincere since the bereaved knows that her visitor has lived through a similar experience. Thus the bereaved will likely feel that her visitor truly understands her dilemma. Second, the visitor provides an appropriate role model for the bereaved. The visitor can supply important information about the appropriate emotional and social responses to bereavement and, perhaps more important, the visiting widow is living proof that one can survive the loss. Being confronted with another well-functioning widow shows that there may be some light at the end of the tunnel. Finally, the widow-to-widow program may be effective because the visitors provide valuable, practical services.

For example, Mrs. Cooperband, the visitor in the Silverman and Cooperband (1975) program, helped one widow find a real estate agent to sell her house, helped another find subsidized housing, and often provided transportation for the recently bereaved. These services are of psychological as well as practical significance. In focusing on the psychological aspects of bereavement, we should not neglect the everyday living problems. As Morgan's (1976) data discussed earlier suggest, solving the mundane problems may do much to alleviate the associated psychological dilemmas.

It is unfortunate that Silverman has not been more systematic and rigorous in assessing the effectiveness of her lay therapy program. For example, it would be interesting to compare the effectiveness of lay versus professional therapy for the bereaved. In such a study, recently bereaved individuals would be assigned to one of three groups:

1   A lay therapy group in which the bereaved would be contacted by carefully screened volunteers who previously went through the bereavement process. These volunteers would be similar to those used by Silverman (1969).

2   A professional therapy group with trained psychologists or psychiatrists.

3   A control group in which patients would receive no special treatment.

Relying on Silverman's description of the effectiveness of her lay therapy program, subjects in the lay-therapy group should experience the best outcomes. Psychological tests and physical indicators of well-being could be used as dependent measures.

Such a study would raise some ethical issues similar to those discussed in Chapter 5. In this case, however, I believe that the benefits outweigh the risks. If it could be demonstrated that lay therapy is an effective treatment procedure, many of the long-term negative consequences of bereavement might be avoided at a very low cost, when compared to professional therapy. Experimental procedures could also be used to determine which of the three factors inherent in lay therapy accounts for the positive outcomes. Further understanding of the bereavement process and advancement in treatment procedures may largely depend on shifting our research strategies to methods that will provide some causal explanation for bereavement phenomena.

7

DEATH
EDUCATION

No matter how much we think, write, or read about death, it is unlikely that we can convince ourselves or most others that death and dying is a positive experience. This book documents many reasons why this is unlikely to happen. At the personal level, it seems that no amount of insight or understanding will totally neutralize the psychological discomfort evoked by thoughts of death, dying, and bereavement. One may ask then, what is the role of manuscripts such as these? This book is justified on two counts.

First, while the information contained in this book is not intended to comfort or convince the reader that death can be a valuable developmental growth experience, it should provide at least partial solutions to some of the problems associated with death and dying. And even for problems where the solutions are not yet available or are inadequate, it may be possible to carry out the necessary research to find solutions. A related and more general goal of this book is to shed enough light on this area to make dying a more predictable and hence controllable process. We have argued throughout this book that the impact of negative events is lessened to the extent that they are predictable and controllable.

For example, giving terminal patients control over the final phase of their lives makes their condition more tolerable. In general, knowledge of and preparation for any critical or traumatic event should decrease its impact. Thus the more the individual knows about death, dying, and bereavement, the better prepared she or he should be to deal with this phase of existence. While preparation may be gained through a variety of means, one of the most effective methods for accomplishing this is through death education courses.

DEATH EDUCATION

Death education can be carried out both informally or formally and can serve several functions. First, death education can offer practical information that may be of great value to practitioners who routinely interact with the dying and bereaved. Second, for the lay person who must inevitably confront the crisis of death and dying, such information may decrease the psychological stress generated by these crises. Third, a death education course may be therapeutic, giving the individual the opportunity to confront and express his or her feelings about death. Each of these functions can be realized through either formal or informal methods, but with either technique the educator should keep in mind the special needs and limitations of his or her pupils.

Death education for children

Perhaps the most salient aspect of death education for the very young is that parents and teachers go to great lengths to avoid defining the concept of death as something irreversible. When a family pet dies, parents frequently rush out to buy a new cat or dog, preferably one that closely resembles the lost pet (Koocher, 1975). When a close relative such as a grandmother dies, it is commonly explained to the child that granny has gone on a long trip. For preschoolers (up to five years of age) this strategy may be appropriate since it is unlikely that the child can understand the concept of death. Most children at this age are unable to differentiate between being out of town and being dead and when told that someone has died may respond with questions such as, where did he go, what is he doing, when will he be back, and so on (Fontenot, 1974; Koocher, 1975; McCurdy, 1974).

The elementary school child (ages 5-9), on the other hand, sees death as final but has trouble understanding causes of death. Death may be personified as a ghost, skeleton, or angel who comes in the night to take people away. By age seven and beyond, according to Koocher (1975), children begin to understand real causes of death and can be told that a pet died because it was run over by a car or that grandmother died of cancer.

Discussions of death have been introduced in some classrooms at the kindergarten and elementary school levels (Koocher, 1975). Children can be asked to make a distinction between living and non-living things, express their personal thoughts on death through art, and discuss the funeral practices and religious beliefs of different cultures. If we can rely on the reports of teachers involved with these classes, the effect of participation appears to be quite positive. Students enjoy the material and at the same time gain insights that typically don't come until much later in life.

Death education for adolescents and adults

Children in junior high school and beyond are old enough to examine death and dying in depth although they are probably not intellectually sophisticated enough to appreciate many of the subtle psychological aspects of the dying process.

Berg and Daugherty (1973) taught a mini-course on death and dying for junior high students at the request of a classmate who lost a parent. The first phase of the course involved assessing students' attitudes toward death and concerns about death. The following are the most commonly asked questions:

1 Does your blood change color when you die?

2 Do people always die with their eyes open?

3 How much does a nice funeral cost?

In the second phase of the course, students were exposed to both fiction and nonfiction reading material to provide them with sufficient background for the remainder of the course. Resource persons representing a wide range of interests were brought in for the final phase of the course. Included were a funeral director, psychologist, artist, musician, doctor, lawyer, war veteran, and religious spokesmen of various faiths. The response to this course was favorable from both parents and students.

At the high school level, a course taught by Fontenot (1974) serves as a good example of how death can be integrated with more traditional subjects. Death was incorporated within an eleventh and twelfth grade English course. The course began with the students reading *Thanatopsis* by Bryant, followed by numerous journal articles and eventually books. Students were asked to write reviews of the journal articles and present an analysis of a book based on answers to the question, "How was death faced by the major character of the book and what insight into human behavior was gained from reading the book?" Class discussions were held focusing on the topics of suicide, euthanasia, funerals, and accepting one's own death as well as the death of others. A survey carried out after the course was completed revealed that 94 out of 96 students agreed that it had been "a worthwhile, meaningful, and helpful experience." Ninety-three of the students agreed that studying death "makes life more precious and meaningful." Perhaps more convincing evidence of the students' involvement is the fact that many did more work (e.g., reading and writing reviews) than required by the teacher.

The largest growth in death education is found at the university level. A course taught by Levitan (*Newsweek*, 1972) at the University of

Maryland is a prototype of such courses. The curriculum covered topics ranging from death in industrial societies to the legal aspects of death and dying to the nature of suicide. Response to the course from the campus community has been overwhelming; it is second only to sex education in popularity. Inevitably someone will combine the two topics and teach a course entitled "Sex and Death."

One of the more unique courses on death and dying is taught at the University of Pittsburgh by Lois Jaffe. Professor Jaffe has terminal leukemia and provides an intensely emotionally involving atmosphere for her students. Participants must confront issues of death and dying not only in the abstract by reading books and journal articles, but they must also learn to deal with a vital, living-yet-dying person. Enrollment is limited in the course to maximize personal interaction, and the demand is always far greater than the available spaces.

Adult and continuing education classes focusing on death and dying are also available in some areas. One of the earliest attempts to teach the public about death was instituted in 1969 by Kastenbaum and Koenig (Thorson, 1974). Their course, entitled "Dying, Death and Lethal Behavior," was offered as a noncredit, seven-week program at Wayne State University in Detroit. The typical participant of the course was either a professional person who was in contact with dying persons or a lay person interested in examining his or her own att'tudes toward death.

A similar course taught at Berry College, located in the mountains of northern Georgia, drew large crowds from the surrounding community. The anticipated attendance the first night was 60 people; 142 turned out, and this number increased each night. The audience consisted roughly of one-third health professionals, one-third persons connected with services for the elderly, and one-third students and community residents (including persons who had recently lost a relative) who were interested in gaining some personal insight into death and dying. The point of view of the latter group is partly represented by a 72-year-old man who expected t > die soon and wanted to know what was going to happen.

Death education for the elderly and terminally ill

Ironically, the opportunities for the segment of the population that might benefit most from death education—that is, the elderly—are very limited. Formal death education courses directed at those closest to death are virtually nonexistent. The paucity of courses is attributable to two factors:

1   There are few courses on any topic available to aged; we should therefore not be surprised to find an absence of courses on death.

2   Educators may assume that given their proximity to death, the aged and seriously ill persons cannot handle a course on death—that is, it might be too upsetting.

The easiest way to test the latter assumption is to offer a course and see what the turnout is.

An example of death education on an informal basis is found at Glen Brae, a retirement community outside of Chicago. As early as 1966, the residents had established what they labeled as "a community of the dying" (Marshall, 1975). Residents were encouraged to voice their thoughts on death and dying, including their own death. Grieving for the dead was kept to a minimum, and the predominant attitude toward death that emerged out of this milieu was that death may not be positive, but it is appropriate.

Death education for the terminally ill is more often designed to serve a therapeutic function than to simply convey information to the patient. The type of interaction Kübler-Ross (1969) provided for her patients is a good example of this type of death education. The goal is to give the patient an opportunity to express the feelings evoked by his or her dilemma. This can and has been achieved through other means as well. Discussion groups for the dying have been organized and a variety of traditional (e.g., psychoanalysis) and new (e.g., LSD drug therapy) therapeutic procedures have been used with terminal patients. To date, there are no data available comparing the effectiveness of any therapeutic procedure to control groups that do not receive therapy. Such studies will undoubtedly be carried out in the near future.

Death education for medical practitioners

Several formal classes on death education for nurses are reported in the literature. Murray (1974) exposed a group of 30 nurses to six 1½-hour sessions on death and dying spaced one week apart. The teaching methods used included lecture-discussion, audio-visual presentations, group dynamics, role playing, and sensitivity training. Templer's (1969) Death Anxiety Scale was administered before and twice after the course was completed. A significant decrease in death anxiety was found when comparing pretest scores to post-test scores that were collected four weeks after the termination of the class. Unfortunately, Murray failed to assess death anxiety in a control group of nurses who were not exposed to the course. Many factors could have caused the decline in death anxiety, such as experimenter demand, maturational processes, and so on. It would have been interesting to determine whether the course affected the nurses' treatment of dying and nondying patients.

Numerous publications have appeared in the last five years aimed at educating medical practitioners in their treatment of dying patients. Among them are Schoenberg, Carr, Peretz, and Kutscher's (1972) book entitled *Psychosocial Aspects of Terminal Care*; Quint's (1967) book entitled *The Nurse and the Dying Patient*; and a recent entry by Epstein (1976) entitled *Nursing the Dying Patient*. In addition, numerous pamphlets are available addressing problems associated with the care of the dying patient (see Epstein, 1976, for a bibliography of such resources).

The status of death education for doctors is more clouded. To shed some light on this issue, Schulz and Sclabassi (1977) mailed a questionnaire to 113 medical schools in the United States asking the following:

1 The number of *required* courses that are exclusively devoted to death and dying and the number of required courses that offer some exposure to this topic.

2 The number of *elective* courses that are exclusively devoted to death and dying and the number of electives that offer some exposure to this topic.

(See Table 7.1.) Sixty-five of the 113 questionnaires mailed were returned. (It should be noted that the cover letter accompanying the questionnaire sent to each school concluded with the statement, "If we do not hear from you, may we assume you do not offer any courses with exposure to the topic of death and dying?" This was done to maximize returns from those schools that offered some exposure to the topic.)

Only one of the questionnaires returned reported not giving their students any exposure to the topic. Slightly over 6 percent of the total number of schools sampled reported having a required course on death and dying while over 40 percent reported having required courses that

TABLE 7.1 *Results of death education survey*
of American medical schools.

	Number	Percent of total*
Required courses		
Schools with at least one course exclusively devoted to death and dying	7	6.2
Schools with at least one course offering some exposure to death and dying	49	43.4
Elective courses		
Schools with at least one course exclusively devoted to death and dying	24	21.2
Schools with at least one course offering some exposure to death and dying	28	24.8

*Questionnaires were sent to 113 medical schools.

touched on this topic. Thus approximately half of the medical schools in the United States currently require of their students at least some exposure to this topic.

Another 46 percent offer elective courses that are either entirely devoted to death and dying or that cover the topic within the context of another course.

The exact nature of the material taught to students is not known. Especially for courses not exclusively devoted to death and dying, the data do not tell us whether the topic is covered in 20 minutes or two weeks. The descriptive information supplied by the respondents indicates that death and dying is typically taught in courses on medical ethics, psychiatry, human values in medicine, family and community health care, and a variety of clerkships.

Given these data, it is difficult to reach an evaluative conclusion on the status of death education in United States medical schools. On the one hand, almost 50 percent of the students have the opportunity to gain exposure to the topic. On the other hand, we have no idea what this exposure is like. The number of required exclusive courses is very small. As a whole, however, it is probably safe to assume that the number of current courses on this topic represents a large increase over years past. And it is likely that curricular development in this area will continue to grow.

CONCLUSION

Death education can serve basically two purposes. It can make the final phase of life more predictable and controllable and it can give the individual the opportunity to understand and express his emotions about death and dying. In short, it can be didactic and/or cathartic. The value of teaching persons how to deal with an often traumatic event in his or her life is indisputable. And to the extent that emotional expression in the context of seminars and courses contributes to this, catharsis may also be valuable. However, the value of the courses aimed at emotional expression of death-related feelings is in need of verification. One can imagine scenarios where such behavior might backfire, leaving the person more anxious and confused than she or he was before participating in such a course. The point is that death education, like most things, can be good or bad depending upon the specific teacher, student, and method of instruction.

BIBLIOGRAPHY

Achte, K. A., and Vauhkonen, M. L. "Cancer and the psyche." *Omega: Journal of Death and Dying* 2(1971): 45-46.

Ader, R. "Experimentally induced gastric lesions: Results and implications of studies in animals." *Advances in Psychosomatic Medicine* 6(1971): 1-39.

Aldrich, C., and Mendkoff, E. "Relocation of the aged and disabled, a mortality study." *Journal of the American Geriatrics Society* 11(1963): 185-194.

Alexander, I. E., and Adlerstein, A. M. "Affective responses to the concept of death in a population of children and early adolescents." *Journal of Genetic Psychology* 93(1958): 167-177.

Alexander, M., and Lester, D. "Fear of death in parachute jumpers." *Perceptual and Motor Skills* 34(1972): 338.

American Medical Association passes "Death with Dignity" resolution. *Science News* 104(1973): 374.

Averill, J. "Personal control over aversive stimuli and its relationship to stress." *Psychological Bulletin* 80(1973): 286-303.

Avorn, J. "Beyond dying." *Harper's Magazine* 246(1973): 56-64.

Ball, T. S., and Volger, R. E. "Uncertain pain and the pain of uncertainty." *Perceptual and Motor Skills* 33(1971): 1195-1203.

Barry, H. "Longevity of outstanding chess players." *Journal of Genetic Psychology* 115(1969): 143-148.

Bartko, J. J.; Patterson, R. D.; and Butler, R. N. "Biomedical and behavioral predictors of survival among normal aged men: A multivariate analysis." In E. Palmore and F. C. Jeffers (Eds.), *Prediction of Life Span*. Lexington, Mass.: D. C. Heath, 1971.

Beard, B. H. "Fear of death and fear of life." *Archives of General Psychiatry* 21(1969): 373-380.

Becker, E. *The Denial of Death*. New York: Free Press, 1973.

Becker, H. "The sorrow of bereavement." *Journal of Abnormal and Social Psychology* 27(1933): 391-409.

Bell, W. "The experimental manipulation of death attitudes: A preliminary investigation." *Omega: Journal of Death and Dying* 6(1975): 199-205.

Bem, D. J. "Self-perception: An alternative interpretation of cognitive dissonance phenomena." *Psychological Review* 74(1967): 183-200.

Berkowitz, B. "Changes in intellect with age: IV. Changes in achievement and survival in older people." *Journal of Genetic Psychology* 107(1965): 3-14.

Berman, A. "Smoking behavior: How is it related to locus of control, death anxiety, and belief in afterlife." *Omega: Journal of Death and Dying* 4(1973): 149-155.

Berman, A. "Belief in afterlife, religion, religiosity, and life-threatening experiences." *Omega: Journal of Death and Dying* 5(1974): 127.

Berman, A., and Hays, J. E. "Relationship between death anxiety, belief in afterlife, and locus of control." *Journal of Consulting and Clinical Psychology* 41(1973): 318.

Binger, C. M.; Feurstein, R. C.; Kushner, J. H.; Zoger, S.; and Mikkelson, C. "Childhood leukemia: Emotional impact on patient and family." *New England Journal of Medicine* 280(1959): 414-418.

Blazer, J. "The relationship between meaning in life and fear of death." *Psychology* 10(1973): 33-34.

Bornstein, P. E.; Clayton, P. J.; Halikas, J. A.; Maurice, W. L.; and Robins, E. "The depression of widowhood after thirteen months." *British Journal of Psychiatry* 122(1973): 561-566.

Bowlby, J. "Grief and mourning in infancy and early childhood." *Psychoanalytic Study of the Child* 15(1960): 9.

Bowlby, J. "Processes of mourning." *International Journal of Psychoanalysis* 44(1961): 317.

Boyar, J. I. "The construction and partial validation of a scale for the measurement of fear of death." Unpublished doctoral dissertation, University of Rochester, Rochester, New York, 1964.

Bozeman, M. F.; Orbach, C. E.; and Sutherland, A. M. "Psychological impact of cancer and its treatment: The adaptation of mothers to the threatened loss of their children through leukemia." *Cancer* 8(1955): 1-19.

Brand, F., and Smith, R. "Life adjustment and relocation of the elderly." *Journal of Gerontology* 29(1974): 336-340.

Brecher, E. M. *Licit and illicit drugs.* Mount Vernon, N.Y.: Consumers Union, 1972.

Brodman, K.; Erdman, A.; and Wolff, H. *Manual for the Cornell medical index.* Ithaca, New York: Cornell University Medical College, 1956.

"Broken heart" syndrome. *Newsweek* 70(1967): 93.

Byrne, D. "Repression-sensitization as a dimension of personality." In B. A. Maher (Ed.), *Progress in Experimental Personality Research, Volume I.* New York: Academic Press, 1964.

Caldwell, D., and Mishara, B. L. "Research on attitudes of medical doctors toward the dying patient: A methodological problem." *Omega: Journal of Death and Dying* 3(1972): 341-346.

Cannon, W. B. "Voodoo death." *American Anthropologist* 44(1942): 169-173.

Cant, G. "How to stay young longer." *McCall's* 102(1974): 87.

Cappon, D. "Attitudes of and toward the dying." *Canadian Medical Association Journal* 87(1969): 693-700.

Casey, R. L.; Masuda, M.; and Holmes, T. H. "Quantitative study of recall of life events." *Journal of Psychosomatic Research* 11(1968): 239-247.

"Cause of death: Fright." *Newsweek,* December 27, 1965, p. 62.

Christ, P. E. I. "Attitudes toward death among a group of acute geriatric psychiatric patients." *Journal of Gerontology* 16(1961): 56-59.

Ciocco, A. "On mortality in husbands and wives." *Human Biology* 12(1940): 508.

Clark, B. "Happiness—the best preventive medicine" *Reader's Digest* 108(1976): 130-132.

Clayton, P. J. "The clinical morbidity of the first year of bereavement: A review." *Comprehensive Psychiatry* 14(1973): (2), 151-157.

Cohen, R., and Parker, O. "Fear of failure and death." *Psychological Reports* 34(1974): 54.

Coleman, J. C. *Abnormal Psychology and Modern Life*. Glenview, Illinois: Scott, Foresman and Co., 1972.

Collett, L., and Lester, D. "Fear of death and fear of dying." *Journal of Psychology* 72(1969): 179-181.

Coppen, A. J. "Depressed states and indolealkylamines." *Advances in Pharmacology* 6B(1968): 283-291.

Corah, N. L., and Boffa, J. "Perceived control, self-observation, and response to aversive stimulation." *Journal of Personality and Social Psychology* 16(1970): 1-4.

Corey, L. G. "An analogue of resistance to death awareness." *Journal of Gerontology* 16(1961): 59-60.

Cox, P. R., and Ford, J. R. "The mortality of widows shortly after widowhood." In T. Ford and G. F. DeJong (Eds.), *Social Demography*. Englewood Cliffs, N. J.: Prentice Hall, 1970.

Crown, B.; O'Donovan, D.; and Thompson, T. G. "Attitudes toward attitudes toward death." *Psychological Reports* 20(1967): 1181-1182.

Crumbaugh, J. C., and Maholick, L. T. "An experimental study in existentialism: The psychometric approach to Frankl's concept of noogenic neurosis." *Journal of Clinical Psychology* 20(1964): 200-207.

David, R. H. "The doctor and the dying patient." *Symposium on the Doctor and the Dying Patient*. University of Southern California School of Medicine, Postgraduate Division of the Department of Psychiatry and Gerontology Center, 1971.

Degner, L. "The relationship between some beliefs held by physicians and their life-prolonging decisions." *Omega: Journal of Death and Dying* 5(1974): 223.

Desjardins, A. V. "What the physician should tell a patient who is affected with malignant lesion." *Journal of the Maine Medical Association* 30(1960): 16-17.

Dickstein, L. "Death concern: Measurement and correlates." *Psychological Reports* 30(1972): 563-571.

Dickstein, L. "Self-report and fantasy correlates of death concern." *Psychological Reports* 32(1975): 147-158.

Diggory, J. C., and Rothman, D. Z. "Values destroyed by death." *Journal of Abnormal and Social Psychology* 63(1961): 205-210.

Dohrenwend, B. S., and Dohrenwend, B. P. *Stressful life events: Their nature and effects.* New York: Wiley, 1974.

Donaldson, P. J. "Denying death: A note regarding some ambiguities in the current discussion." *Omega: Journal of Death and Dying* 3(1972): 285-290.

Dublin, L. I. *The facts of life—From birth to death.* New York: Macmillan, 1951.

Durlak, J. "Measurement of the fear of death: An examination of some existing scales." *Journal of Clinical Psychology* 28(1972a): 545-547.

Durlak, J. "Relationship between individual attitudes toward life and death." *Journal of Consulting and Clinical Psychology* 38(1972b): 463.

Durlak, J. "Relationship between various measures of death concern and fear of death." *Journal of Consulting and Clinical Psychology* 41(1973a): 162.

Durlak, J. "Relationship between attitudes toward life and death among elderly women." *Developmental Psychology* 8(1973b): 146.

Eisendrath, R. M. "The role of grief and fear in the death of kidney transplant patients." *American Journal of Psychiatry* 126(1969): 381-387.

Eliot, T. D. "A step toward the social psychology of bereavement." *Journal of Abnormal and Social Psychology* 27(1933): 380-390.

Epstein, C. *Nursing the Dying Patient.* Reston, Virginia: Reston, 1975.

Faunce, W. A., and Fulton, R. L. "The sociology of death: A neglected area of research." *Social Forces* 36(1958): 205-209.

Feifel, H. "Religious conviction and fear of death among the healthy and the terminally ill." *Journal for the Scientific Study of Religion* 13(1974): 353-360.

Feifel, H., and Branscomb, A. "Who's afraid of death?" *Journal of Abnormal Psychology* 81(1973): 282-288.

Feifel, H.; Freilich, J.; and Hermann, L. "Death fear in dying heart and cancer patients." *Journal of Psychosomatic Research* 17(1973): 161-166.

Feifel, H.; Hanson, S.; Jones, R.; and Edwards, L. "Physicians consider death." *Proceedings of the 75th Annual Convention of the American Psychological Association* 2(1967): 201-202.

Feifel, H., and Heller, J. "Normalcy, illness and death." In *Proceedings of the Third World Congress of Psychiatry.* Toronto: University of Toronto Press, 1960.

Feifel, H., and Hermann, L. "Fear of death in the mentally ill." *Psychological Reports* 33(1973): 931-938.

Fitts, W. T., and Ravdin, I. S. "What Philadelphia physicians tell patients with cancer." *Journal of the American Medical Association* 153(1953): 901-904.

Fontenot, C. "The subject no one teaches." *English Journal* 63(1974): (2) 62-63.

Frankl, V. E. *The Doctor and the Soul.* New York: Knopf, 1965.

Fredrick, J. F. "Physiological reactions induced by grief." *Omega: Journal of Death and Dying* 2(1971): 71-75.

Friedman, M., and Rosenman, R. H. *Type A Behavior and Your Heart.* New York: Knopf, 1974.

Friedman, S. B., and Zaris, D. "Behavioral observations of parents anticipating the death of a child." *Pediatrics* 32(1963): 610-625.

Fulton, R. "Discussion of a symposium on attitudes toward death in older persons." *Journal of Gerontology* 16(1961): 44-66.

Fulton, R. "Death, grief, and social recuperation." *Omega: Journal of Death and Dying* 1(1970): 23-28.

Galston, A. W. "In search of the anti-aging cocktail." *Natural History* 84(1975): 14-19.

Gauthier, Y. "The mourning reaction of a ten-year-old boy." *Canadian Psychiatric Association Journal (Supplement)* 11(1966): 307-308.

Gertler, R., and Ferneau, E. "The first year resident in psychiatry: How he sees the psychiatric patient's attitudes toward death and dying." *International Journal of Social Psychiatry* 21(1974-75): 4-6.

Gertler, R.; Ferneau, E.; and Raynes, A. "Attitudes toward death and dying on a drug addiction unit." *International Journal of the Addictions* 8(1973): 265-272.

Glaser, B. G., and Strauss, A. L. *Awareness of Dying.* Chicago: Aldine, 1965.

Glass, D. C., and Singer, J. E. *Urban Stress.* New York: Academic Press, 1972.

Glick, I. O.; Weiss, R. S.; and Parkes, C. M. *The First Year of Bereavement.* New York: Wiley, 1974.

Golan, N. "Wife to widow to woman." *Social Work* 20(1975) 369-374.

Goldfarb, A. I. "Predicting mortality in the institutionalized aged." *Archives of General Psychiatry* 21(1969): 172-176.

Golding, S. L.; Atwood, G. E.; and Goodman, R. A. "Anxiety and two cognitive forms of resistance to the idea of death." *Psychological Reports* 18(1966): 359-364.

Goodman, L. "Winning the race with death, fear of death, and creativity." Symposium, *American Psychological Association Convention,* Chicago, Illinois, 1975.

Gorer, G. *Death, Grief and Mourning in Contemporary Britain.* London: Cresset, 1965.

Granick, S. "Cognitive aspects of longevity." In E. Palmore and F. C. Jeffers (Eds.), *Prediction of Life Span.* Lexington, Mass.: D. C. Heath, 1971.

Granville-Grossman, K. L. "Early bereavement and schizophrenia." *British Journal of Psychiatry* 112(1966): 1027-1034.

Gutman, G. M., and Herbert, C. P. Mortality rates among relocated extended-care patients. *Journal of Gerontology* 31(1976): 352-357.

Hall, G. S. *Senescence.* New York: Appleton, 1922.

Hamovitch, M. B. *The Parent and the Fatally Ill Child*. Duarte, Calif.: City of Hope Medical Center, 1964.

Handal, P. J. "Development of a controlled repression-sensitization scale and some preliminary validity data." *Journal of Clinical Psychology* 29(1973): 486-487.

Handal, P.J., and Rychlak, J. F. "Curvilinearity between dream content and death anxiety and the relationship of death anxiety to repression-sensitization." *Journal of Abnormal Psychology* 77(1971): 11-16.

Hendin, D. *Death as a Fact of Life*. New York: Norton, 1973.

Heyman, D. K., and Gianturco, D. T. "Long-term adaptation by the elderly to bereavement," *Journal of Gerontology* 28(1973): 359-362.

Hinton, J. *Dying*. Baltimore: Penguin Books, 1967.

Hinton, J. M. "The physical and mental distress of the dying." *Quarterly Journal of Medicine* 32(1963): 1-21.

Hoerr, S. O. "Thoughts on what to tell the patient with cancer." *Cleveland Clinic Quarterly* 30(1963): 11-16.

Holden, C. "Hospices: For the dying, relief from pain and fear." *Science* 193(1976): 389-391.

Horn, J. "Regriefing: A way to end pathological mourning." *Psychology Today* 1(1974): (2), 184.

House, J. S. "Occupational stress as a precursor to coronary disease." In W. D. Gentry and R. B. Williams, Jr. (Eds.), *Psychological Aspects of Myocardial Infarction and Coronary Care*. Saint Louis: Mosby, 1975.

Hyman, G. A. "Medical needs of the bereaved family." In A. H. Kutscher (Ed.), *But Not to Lose*. New York: Frederick Fall, 1969.

Iammarino, N. K. "Relationship between death anxiety and demographic variables." *Psychological Reports* 17(1975): 262.

Janis, I. L. *Psychological Stress*. New York: Wiley, 1958.

Janis, I. L., and Leventhal, H. "Human reaction to stress." In E. F. Borgatta and W. W. Lambert (Eds.), *Handbook of Personality Theory and Research*. Chicago: Rand McNally, 1968.

Jeffers, F. C.; Nichols, C. R.; and Eisdorfer, C. "Attitudes of older persons to death." *Journal of Gerontology* 16(1961): 53-56.

Jenkins, C. D. "Psychologic and social precursors of coronary disease." *New England Journal of Medicine* 284(1971): 244-255; 307-317.

Jenkins, C.D. "The coronary-prone personality." In W. D. Gentry and R. B. Williams (Eds.), *Psychological Aspects of Myocardial Infarction and Coronary Care*. Saint Louis: Mosby, 1975.

Jones, E. E., and Sigall, H. "The bogus pipeline: A new paradigm for measuring affect and attitude." *Psychological Bulletin* 76(1971): 349-364.

Kalish, R. A. "Some variables in death attitudes." *Journal of Social Psychology* 59(1963): 137-145.

Kalish, R. A. "Added years: Social issues and consequences." In E. Palmore and F. C. Jeffers (Eds.), *Prediction of Life Span*. Lexington, Mass.: D. C. Heath, 1971.

Kalish, R., and Reynolds, D. "Widows view death." *Omega: Journal of Death and Dying* 5(1974): 187.

Kannel, W. B. "Habits and heart disease mortality." In E. Palmore and F. C. Jeffers (Eds.), *Prediction of Life Span*. Lexington, Mass.: D. C. Heath, 1971.

Kasindorf, J. "Eat, drink and live to a ripe old age." *McCall's* 101(1974): 39.

Kasper, A. M. "The doctor and death." In H. Feifel (Ed.), *The Meaning of Death*. New York: McGraw-Hill, 1959.

Kasteler, J.; Gary, R.; and Carruth, M. "Involuntary relocation of the elderly." *Gerontologist* 8(1968): 276-279.

Kastenbaum, R., and Aisenberg, R. *The Psychology of Death*. New York: Springer, 1972.

Kastenbaum, R., and Aisenberg, R. "Death as a thought." In E. S. Schneidman (Ed.), *Death: Current Perspectives*. Palo Alto, Calif.: Mayfield, 1976.

Kastenbaum, R., and Briscoe, L. "The street corner: A laboratory for the study research procedure in gerontology." In D. P. Kent, R. Kastenbaum, and S. 6(1975): 33.

Kastenbaum, R., and Costa, P. T. "Psychological perspectives on death." In M. R. Rosenzweig and L. W. Porter (Eds.) *Annual Review of Psychology* 8(1977): 225-249.

Kastenbaum, R., and Kastenbaum, B. S. "Hope, survival, and the caring environment." In E. Palmore and F. C. Jeffers (Eds.), *Prediction of Life Span*. Lexington, Mass.: D. C. Heath, 1971.

Kastenbaum, R., and Weisman, A. D. "The psychological autopsy as a research procedure in gerontology." In D. P. Dent, R. Kastenbaum, and S. Sherwood (Eds.), *Research Planning and Action for the Elderly*. New York: Behavioral Publications, 1972.

Kavanaugh, R. E. *Facing Death*. Baltimore, Md.: Penguin Books, 1974.

Kelly, W. D., and Friesen, S. R. "Do cancer patients want to be told?" *Surgery* (1950) 822-826.

Killian, E. C. "Effect of geriatric transfers on mortality rates." *Social Work* 15(1970): 19-26.

Kimball, C. P. "Psychological responses to the experience of open heart surgery: I" *Journal of Psychiatry* 126(1969): 348-359.

Kits van Heijningen, H., and Teurniet, N. "Psychosomatic factors in acute myocardial infarction." *International Journal of Psychoanalysis* 47(1966). 370-374.

Kleemeier, R. W. "Intellectual change in the senium on death and the I.Q." *Presidential address, American Psychological Association*, 1961.

Kleemeier, R. W. "Intellectual change in the senium." *Proceedings of the Social Statistics Section of the American Statistical Association* (1962) 290-295.

Koocher, G. P. "Why isn't the gerbil moving anymore?" *Children Today* 4(1975): (1), 18-21, 36.

Kostolansky, R. "Factor analysis of physiological age, social variables and cognitive load in elderly women." *Studia Psychologica* 4(1973): 328-334.

Kraus, A. S., and Lilienfeld, A. M. "Some epidemiological aspects of the high mortality rate in the young widowed." *Journal of Chronic Disease* 10(1959): 207-217.

Krieger, S.; Epsting, F.; and Leitner, L. M. "Personal constructs, threat, and attitudes toward death." *Omega: Journal of Death and Dying* 5(1974): 299.

Kritsikis, S. P.; Heinemann, A. L.; and Eitner, S. "Die angina pectoris in aspektihrer korrelation mit biologisher disposition, psychologischen und soziologischen einflussfaktoren." *Deutsche Gesundheitswesen* 23(1968): 1878-1885.

Kübler-Ross, E. *On Death and Dying*. New York: Macmillan, 1969.

Kübler-Ross, E. "Therapy with the terminally ill." In E. S. Schneidman (Ed.), *Death: Current Perspectives*. Palo Alto, Calif.: Mayfield, 1976.

Kutscher, A. H.; Schoenberg, B.; and Carr, A. C. "Thanatology as related to dentistry." *Journal of the American Dental Association* 81(1970): 1373-1377.

Lasagna, L. "The doctor and the dying patient." *Journal of Chronic Disease* 22(1969): 65-68.

Leaf, A. "Getting old." *Scientific American* 229(1973): (3), 45-52.

Leaf, A. *Youth in Old Age*. New York: McGraw-Hill, 1975.

Lerner, M. "When, why, and where people die." In E. S. Shneidman (Ed.), *Death: Current perspectives*. Palo Alto, Calif.: Mayfield, 1976.

"A lesson in dying." *Life*, December 13, 1968, *65*, pp. 107-108.

LeShan, L. "A basic psychological orientation apparently associated with malignant disease." *Psychiatric Quarterly* 35(1961): 314-330.

Lester, D. "Fear of death of suicide persons." *Psychological Reports* 20(1967a): 1077-1078.

Lester, D. "Experimental and correlational studies of the fear of death." *Psychological Bulletin* 67(1967b): 27-36.

Lester, D. "Sex differences in attitudes toward death: A replication." *Psychological Reports* 28(1971): 754.

Lester, D. "Studies in death attitudes." *Psychological Reports* 30(1972): 440.

Lester, D.; Getty, C.; and Kneisl, C. "Attitudes of nursing students and nursing faculty toward death." *Nursing Research* 23(1974): 50-53.

Lester, D., and Lester, G. "Fear of death, fear of dying, and threshold differences for death words and neutral words. "*Omega: Journal of Death and Dying* 1(1970): 175-179.

Lester, D., and Templer, D. "Resemblance of parent-child death anxiety as a function of age and sex of child." *Psychological Reports* 31(1972): 750.

Leviton, D. "Death education and change in students' attitudes." Final Research Report, National Institute of Mental Health Research Grant MH 21974-01, Washington, D. C., 1973.

Lieberman, M. A. "Relationships of mortality rates to entrance to a home for the aged." *Geriatrics* 16(1961): 515-519.

Lieberman, M. A. "Psychological correlates of impending death: Some preliminary observations." *Journal of Gerontology* 20(1965): 181-190.

Lieberman, M. A. "Some issues in studying psychological predictors of survival." In E. Palmore and F. C. Jeffers (Eds.), *Prediction of Life Span.* Lexington, Mass.: D. C. Heath, 1971.

Lief, H. I., and Fox, R. C. "Training for detached concern in medical students." In H. I. Lief and N. R. Lief (Eds.), *The Psychological Basis of Medical Practice.* New York: Harper & Row, 1963.

Lindemann, E. "Symptomatology and management of acute grief." *American Journal of Psychiatry* 101(1944): 141-148.

Lindzey, G.; Lykken, D. T.; and Winston, H. D. "Infantile trauma, genetic factors, and adult temperament." *Journal of Abnormal and Social Psychology* 61(1960): 7-14.

Lirette, W. L.; Palmer, R. L.; Ibarra, I. D.; Kroenig, P. M.; and Gaines, R. K. "Management of patients with terminal cancer." *Postgraduate Medicine* 46(1969): 145-149.

Litin, E. M. "What shall we tell the cancer patient? A psychiatrist's view." *Proceedings of the Mayo Clinic* 35(1960): 247-250.

Livingston, P. B., and Zimet, C. N. "Death anxiety, authoritarianism and choice of specialty in medical students." *Journal of Nervous and Mental Disease* 140(1965): 222-230.

Lowry, R. "Male-female differences in attitudes toward death." Unpublished doctoral dissertation, Brandeis University, 1965.

Lucas, R. "A comparative study of measures of general anxiety and death anxiety among three medical groups including patient and wife." *Omega: Journal of Death and Dying* 5(1974): 233.

Madigan, F. "Role satisfaction and length of life in a closed population." *American Journal of Sociology* 67(1962): 640-649.

Maguire, D. C. "Death by chance, death by choice." *Atlantic* 233(1974a): (1), 57-65.

Maguire, D. C. "Death, legal and illegal." *Atlantic* 233(1974b): (2), 72-85.

Markus, E.; Blenkner, J.; Bloom, M.; and Downs, T. "Some factors and their association with post-relocation mortality among institutionalized aged persons." *Journal of Gerontology* 27(1972): 376-382.

Markusen, E., and Fulton, R. "Childhood bereavement and behavior disorder: A critical review." *Omega: Journal of Death and Dying* 2(1971): 107-117.

Marshall, V. "Socialization for impending death in a retirement village." *American Journal of Sociology* 80(1975): 1124-1144.

Mathison, J. "A cross-cultural view of widowhood." *Omega: Journal of Death and Dying* 1(1970): 201-218.

McCurdy, J. "Death studies should begin with 'very young.'" *The Times Educational Supplement* April 26, 1974, **12**.

McKegney, F., and Lange, P. "The decision to no longer live on chronic dialysis." *American Journal of Psychiatry* 128(1971): 267.

McQuade, W. "What stress can do to you." *Fortune* 85(1972): (1), 102-141.

Mechanic, D. "Discussion of research programs on relations between stressful life events and episodes of physical illness." In B. S. Dohrenwend and B. P. Dohrenwend (Eds.), *Stressful Life Events: Their Nature and Effects.* New York: Wiley, 1974.

Melges, F. T., and Bowlby, J. "Types of hopelessness in psycho-pathological process." *Archives of General Psychiatry* 20(1969): 690-699.

Metropolitan Life Insurance Company. "College men long lived." *Statistical Bulletin* 13(1932): (8).

Metropolitan Life Insurance Company. "Longevity of prominent men." *Statistical Bulletin* 49(1968).

Meyer, J. E. *Death & Neurosis.* New York: International Universities Press, 1975.

Mishara, B.; Baker, H.; and Kostin, I. "Do people who seek less environmental stimulation avoid thinking about the future and their deaths?" *Proceedings of the Annual Convention of the APA* 7(1972): 667-668.

Moody, R. A. *Life after life.* Atlanta: Mockingbird Books, 1975.

Morgan, L. A. "A re-examination of widowhood and morale." *Journal of Gerontology* 31(1976): 687-695.

Morris, W. (Ed.), *The American Heritage Dictionary of the English Language.* Boston: Houghton Mifflin, 1969.

Murray, P. "Death education and its effects on the death anxiety level of nurses." *Psychological Reports* 35(1974): 1250.

Nagy, M. "The child's view of death." In Feifel, H. (Ed.), *The Meaning of Death.* New York: McGraw-Hill, 1959.

Nash, M. L. "Reflection-action model designed for response to human qualities of persons in their terminal phase of life." Unpublished manuscript, Carlow College, 1975.

Natterson, J. M., and Knudson, A. C. "Observation concerning fear of death in fatally ill children and mothers." *Psychosomatic Medicine* 22(1960): 456-465.

Neale, R. E. "Between the nipple and the everlasting arms." *Archives of the Foundation of Thanatology* 3(1971): 21-30.

Nelson, L. D., and Nelson, C. C. "A factor analytic inquiry into the multidimensionality of death anxiety." *Omega: Journal of Death and Dying* 6(1975): 171-178.

Nogas, C.; Schweitzer, K.; and Grumet, J. "An investigation of death anxiety, sense of competence, and need for achievement." *Omega: Journal of Death and Dying* 5(1974): 245.

Noyes, R., Jr. "The art of dying." *Perspectives in Biology and Medicine* 14(1971): 432-447.

Oken, D. "What to tell cancer patients." *Journal of the American Medical Association* 175(1961), 1120-1128.

Osarchuck, M., and Tatz, S. "Effect of induced fear of death on belief in afterlife." *Journal of Personality and Social Psychology* 27(1973): 256-260.

Palmore, E. Health practices, illness, and longevity. In E. Palmore and F. C. Jeffers (Eds.), *Prediction of Life Span*. Lexington, Mass.: D. C. Heath, 1971a.

Palmore, E. The relative importance of social factors in predicting longevity. In E. Palmore and F. C. Jeffers (Eds.) *Prediction of Life Span*. Lexington, Mass.: D. C. Heath, 1971b.

Pandey, R. E. "Factor analytic study of attitudes toward death among college students." *International Journal of Social Psychiatry* 21(1974-75): 7-11.

Pandey, R. E., and Templer, D. "Use of the death anxiety scale in an inter-racial setting." *Omega: Journal of Death and Dying* 3(1972): 127-130.

Paris, J., and Goodstein, L. "Responses to death and sex stimulus materials as a function of repression-sensitization." *Psychological Reports* 19(1966): 1283-1291.

Parkes, C. M. Effects of bereavement on physical and mental health—a study of medical records of widows. *British Journal of Medicine* 2(1964): 274-279.

Parkes, C. M. *Bereavement: Studies of Grief in Adult Life*. New York: International Universities Press, 1972.

Pauling, L. "Five ways to live longer." *Saturday Evening Post* 240(1974): 26-28.

Pearlman, J.; Stotsky, B. A.; and Dominick, J. R. "Attitudes toward death among nursing home personnel." *Journal of Genetic Psychology* 114(1969): 63-75.

Pervin, L. A. "The need to predict and control under conditions of threat." *Journal of Personality* 31(1963): 570-587.

Pfeiffer, E. Physical, psychological, and social correlates of survival in old age. In E. Palmore and F. C. Jeffers (Eds.), *Prediction of Life Span*. Lexington, Mass.: D. C. Heath, 1971.

Phillips, D. P., and Feldman, K. A. "A dip in deaths before ceremonial occasions: Some new relationships between social integration and mortality." *American Sociological Review* 38(1973): 678-696.

Proxmire, W. *You Can Do It!*. New York: Simon and Schuster, 1973.

Proxmire, W. Preface. In K. H. Cooper, *Aerobics*. New York: Bantam Books, 1976.

Quint, J. C. *The Nurse and the Dying Patient*. Chicago: Aldine, 1967.

Rahe, R. H. "Life crisis and health change." In R. A. May Philip and J. R. Wittenborn (Eds.), *Psychotropic Drug Response: Advances in Prediction.* Springfield, Ill.: Thomas, 1969.

Rahe, R. H., and Lind, E. "Psychosocial factors and sudden cardiac death: A pilot study." *Journal of Psychosomatic Research* 15(1971): 19-24.

Rahe, R. H., and Paasikivi, J. "Psychosocial factors and myocardial infarction.II. An out-patient study in Sweden." *Journal of Psychosomatic Research* 15(1971): 33-39.

Rahe, R. H.; Romo, M.; Bennett, L. K.; and Siltanen, P. "Finnish subjects' recent life changes, myocardial infarction, and abrupt coronary death." Unit Report 72-40, *U. S. Navy Medical Neuropsychiatric Research Unit,* San Diego, 1973.

Ray, J. J., and Najman, J. "Death anxiety and death acceptance: A preliminary approach." *Omega: Journal of Death and Dying* 5(1974): 311.

"How recession can kill." *Newsweek* 76(1970): p. 62.

Rennick, D. "What should physicians tell cancer patients?" *New Medical Material* 2(1960): 51-53.

Rheingold, J. C. *The Mother, Anxiety, and Death.* Boston: Little Brown, 1967.

Rhudick, P. J., and Dibner, A. S. "Age, personality and health correlates of death concern in normal aged individuals." *Journal of Gerontology* 16(1961): 44-49.

Richter, C. P. "On the phenomenon of sudden death in animals and man." *Psychosomatic Medicine* 19(1957): 191-198.

Riegel, K. F. "The prediction of death and longevity in longitudinal research." In E. Palmore and F. C. Jeffers (Eds.). *Prediction of Life Span.* Lexington, Mass.: D. C. Heath, 1971.

Rose, C. L. "Review of the literature: Social factors." In C. L. Rose and B. Bell (Eds.). *Predicting Longevity.* Lexington, Mass.: D. C. Heath, 1971.

Rose, C. L., and Bell, B. (Eds.). *Predicting Longevity.* Lexington, Mass.: D. C. Heath, 1971.

Rose, C. R. "Social correlates of longevity." In R. E. Kastenbaum (Ed.), *New Thoughts on Old Age.* New York: Springer, 1964.

Rosenman, R. H. et al. "Coronary heart disease in the Western Collaborative Group Study: A follow-up experience of 4½ years." *Journal of Chronic Diseases* 23(1970): 173.

Ross, M. H., and Bras, G. "Food preference and length of life." *Science* 190(1975): 165-167.

Rothstein, S. H. "Aging awareness and personalization of death in the young and middle adult years." Unpublished doctoral dissertation, University of Chicago, 1967.

Rotter, J. B. "Generalized expectancies for internal vs. external control of reinforcements." *Psychological Monographs* 80(1966): (Whole No. 609)

Russek, H. I. "Emotional stress and coronary heart disease in American physicians, dentists, and lawyers." *American Journal of Medical Science* 243(1962): 716.

Russek, H. I. "Stress, tobacco and coronary disease in North American professional groups." *Journal of the American Medical Association* 192(1965): 189-194.

Sales, S. M. "Organizational role as a risk factor in coronary disease." *Administrative Science Quarterly* 14(1969): 324-336.

Samp, R. J., and Curreri, A. R. "Questionnaire survey on public cancer education obtained from cancer patients and their families." *Cancer* 10(1957): 382-384.

Sarnoff, I., and Corwin, S. M. "Castration anxiety and the fear of death." *Journal of Personality* 27(1959): 374-385.

Schildkraut, J. J., and Kety, S. S. "Biogenic amines and emotion." *Science* 156(1967): 21-30.

Shneidman, E. S. "The death certificate." In E. S. Shneidman (Ed.). *Death: Current perspectives*. Palo Alto, Calif.: Mayfield, 1976.

Shneidman, E. S. "Postvention and the survivor-victim," In E. S. Shneidman (Ed.). *Death: Current perspectives*. Palo Alto, Calif.: Mayfield, 1976.

Schoenberg, B. "A survey of the advice of physicians for the bereaved." *General Practitioner* 40(1969): 105-110.

Schoenberg, B; Carr, A. C.; Peretz, D; and Kutscher, A. H. *Psychosocial Aspects of Terminal Care*. New York: Columbia University Press, 1972.

Schulz, R. "Effects of control and predictability on the physical and psychological well-being of the institutionalized aged." *Journal of Personality and Social Psychology* 33(1976a) 563-573.

Schulz, R. "Some life and death consequences of perceived control." In J. S. Carroll and J. W. Payne (Eds.). *Cognition and Social Behavior*. Hillsdale, N. J.: Erlbaum, 1976b.

Schulz, R., and Aderman, D. "Effects of residential change on the temporal distance to death of terminal cancer patients." *Omega: Journal of Death and Dying* 4(1973): 157-162.

Schulz, R., and Aderman, D. "Clinical research and the stages of dying." *Omega: Journal of Death and Dying* 5(1974): 137-143.

Schulz, R., and Aderman, D. "Physicians' death anxiety and survival of patients." Unpublished manuscript, 1977.

Schulz, R.; Aderman, D.; and Manko, G. "Attitudes toward death: The effects of different methods of questionnaire administration." Paper presented at the meeting of the Eastern Psychological Association, New York, April, 1976.

Schulz, R., and Brenner, G. "Relocation of the aged: A review and theoretical analysis." *Journal of Gerontology* 32(1977): 323-333.

Schulz, R., and Shelton, E. "Cognitive and behavioral mediators of the stress-illness relationship." Unpublished manuscript, Carnegie-Mellon University, 1976.

Seligman, M. E. P. *Helplessness.* San Francisco: Freeman, 1975.

Seligmann, J. "A right to die." *Newsweek* 88(1976): (15), 52.

Selvey, C. "Concerns about death in relation to sex, dependency, guilt about hostility, and feelings of powerlessness." *Omega: Journal of Death and Dying* 4(1973): 209-219.

Selye, H. *The Physiology and Pathology of Exposure to Stress.* Montreal: Acta, 1950.

Shand, A. E. *The Foundations of Character.* London: Macmillan, 1920.

Shearer, R. E. "Religious belief and attitudes toward death." *Dissertation Abstracts International* 33(1973): 3292-3293.

Sherwin, B. L. "Jewish views of euthanasia." In M. Kohl (Ed.), *Beneficent Euthanasia.* Buffalo, N.Y.: Prometheus Books, 1975.

Shideler, M. M. "Coup de grace." *Christian Century* 83(1966): 1503-1506.

Shrut, S. D. "Attitudes towards old age and health." *Mental Hygiene* 42(1958): 259-266.

Shusterman, L., and Sechrest, L. "Attitudes or RNs toward death in a general hospital." *Psychiatry in Medicine* 4(1973): 411-426.

Silverman, P. R. "The widow-to-widow program. An experiment in preventive intervention." *Mental Hygiene* 53(1969): 333-337.

Silverman, P. R., and Cooperband, A. "On widowhood: Mutual help and the elderly widow." *Journal of Geriatric Psychiatry* 8(1975): 9-27.

Snyder, M.; Gertler, R.; and Ferneau, E. "Changes in nursing students' attitudes toward death and dying: A measurement of curriculum integration effectiveness." *International Journal of Social Psychiatry* 19(1973): 294-298.

Staub, E.; Tursky, B.; and Schwartz, G. E. "Self-control and predictability: Their effects on reactions to aversive stimuli." *Journal of Personality and Social Psychology* 18(1971): 157-162.

Stotland, E. *The Psychology of Hope.* San Francisco: Jossey-Bass, 1969.

Strehler, B. L. "Making the machine run longer." *Harper's* 246(1973): (1477), 8.

Stroop, J. R. "Factors affecting speed in serial verbal reactions." *Psychological Monographs* 50(1938): 38-48.

Swenson, W. M. "Attitudes toward death in an aged population." *Journal of Gerontology* 16(1961): 49-52.

Tarter, R.; Templer, D.; and Perley, R. "Death anxiety in suicide attempters." *Psychological Reports* 34(1974): 895-897.

Templer, D. "The construction and validation of a death anxiety scale." *Journal of General Psychology* 82(1970): 165-177.

Templer, D. "Death anxiety as related to depression and health of retired persons." *Journal of Gerontology* 26(1971a): 521-523.

Templer, D. "The relationship between verbalized and nonverbalized death anxiety." *Journal of Genetic Psychology* 119(1971b): 211-214.

Templer, D. "Death anxiety in religiously very involved persons." *Psychological Reports* 31(1972a): 361-362.

Templer, D. "Death anxiety: Extraversion, neuroticism, and cigarette smoking." *Omega: Journal of Death and Dying* 3(1972b): 53-56.

Templer, D.; Lester, D.; and Ruff, C. "Fear of death and femininity." *Psychological Reports* 35(1974): 530.

Templer, D., and Ruff, C. "Death anxiety scale means, standard deviations, and embedding." *Psychological Reports* 29(1971): 173-174.

Templer, D.; Ruff, C; and Franks, C. "Death anxiety: Age, sex and parental resemblance in diverse populations." *Developmental Psychology* 4(1971): 108.

Templer, D.; Ruff, C.; and Simpson, K. "Alleviation of high death anxiety with symptomatic treatment of depression." *Psychological Reports* 35(1974): 216.

Terman, L. M., and Oden, M. H. *The Gifted Child Grows Up. Genetic Studies of Genius*, Vol. IV. Stanford: Stanford University Press, 1959.

Theorell, T. "Life events before and after the onset of a premature myocardial infarction." In B. S. Dohrenwend and B. P. Dohrenwend (Eds.), *Stressful Live Events: Their Nature and Effects*. New York: Wiley, 1974.

Theorell, T., and Rahe, R. H. "Psychosocial factors and myocardial infarction. I. An inpatient study in Sweden." *Journal of Psychosomatic Research* 15(1971): 25-31.

Thorson, J. A. "Continuing education in death and dying." *Adult Leadership* 23(1974): (5), 141-144.

Tolor, A., and Reznikoff, M. "Relationship between insight, repression-sensitization, internal-external control, and death anxiety." *Journal of Abnormal Psychology* 72(1967): 426-430.

Veatch, R. M. "Brain death." In E. S. Shneidman (Ed.), *Death: Current Perspectives*. Palo Alto, Calif.: Mayfield, 1976.

Verwoerdt, A., and Elmore, J. L. "Psychological reactions in fatal illness. I. The prospect of impending death." *Journal of the American Geriatrics Society* 15(1967): 9-19.

Vinokur, A., and Selzer, M. L. "Desirable versus undesirable life events: Their relationship to stress and mental distress." *Journal of Personality and Social Psychology* 32(1975): 329-337.

Wahl, C. W. "The physician's management of the dying patient." In J. Masserman (Ed.), *Current Psychiatric Therapies*. New York: Gruen and Stratton, 1962.

Wahl, C. W. "Should a patient be told the truth?" In A. H. Kutscher (Ed.), *But Not to Lose*. New York: Fredrick Fell, 1969.

Wainwright, L. "A profound lesson for the living." *Life* 67(1969): Nov. 21, 36-43.

Weisman, A. D., and Hackett, T. P. "Predilection to death." *Psychosomatic Medicine* 23(1961): 232-256.

Weisman, A. D., and Kastenbaum, R. "The psychological autopsy; a study of the terminal phase of life." *Community Mental Health Journal* (1968) Monograph No. 4.

Weiss, J. M. "Somatic effects of predictable and unpredictable shock." *Psychosomatic Medicine* 32(1970): 397-408.

Weiss, J. M. "Effects of coping behavior in different warning signal conditions on stress pathology in rats." *Journal of Comparative and Physiological Psychology* 77(1971): 1-30.

Weiss, J. M. "Psychological factors in stress and disease." *Scientific American* 226(1972): 104-113.

Wheeler, A. L. "The dying person: A deviant in the medical subculture." Paper presented at the annual meeting of the Southern Sociological Society, Atlanta, Georgia, April, 1973.

Wittmaier, B. "The impact of a death course." Unpublished manuscript, Kirkland College, New York, 1975.

Wyrsch, J. "Should we inform the patient about the cancer diagnosis?" *Schweizerische Medizinische Wochenschrift* 92(1962): 1577-1588.

Yamamoto, J. "Cultural factors in loneliness, death, and separation." *Medical Times* 98(1970): 177-183.

Yeaworth, R.; Kapp, F.; and Winget, C. "Attitudes of nursing students toward the dying patient." *Nursing Research* 23(1974): 20-24.

Young, M.; Bernard, B; and Wallis, C. "The mortality of widowers." In T. Ford and G. F. DeJong (Eds.), *Social Demography*. Englewood Cliffs, N.J.: Prentice Hall, 1970.

Zilboorg, G. "Fear of death." *Psychoanalytic Quarterly* 12(1943): 465-475.

INDEX

Date Due